A CAMEL'S STORY

A SEARCH for the MESSIAH

by Sandy Hanson

illustrations by Kristi Delage and Sandy Hanson

God bless your Journey
Sandy Hanson

DEDICATED to

Our precious children ~ May you know Jesus as your Lord and Savior and share the message of His Great love with your generations. Search for Him with all your heart!

Copyright © 2005; 2011 Sandra (Homan) Hanson
All rights reserved. No part of this book may be reproduced, stored in a retrieval system, or transmitted in any form or by any means, electronic, photocopying or otherwise, except for the inclusion of brief quotations in review, without the prior written consent from the author.

Scripture is taken from the LIFE APPLICATION BIBLE, NEW INTERNATIONAL VERSION (NIV); copyright © 1988, 1989, 1990, 1991 by Tyndale House Publishers, Inc., Wheaton, IL 60189; published by Tyndale House Publishers, Inc. all rights reserved

Notes and Bible helps taken from the LIFE APPLICATION BIBLE, NEW INTERNATIONAL VERSION (NIV); copyright © 1988, 1989, 1990, 1991 by Tyndale House Publishers, Inc., Wheaton, IL 60189; published by Tyndale House Publishers, Inc. all rights reserved

Additional information and resources taken from:
<u>1000 Things You Should Know About Wild Animals</u> – copyright © Miles Kelly Publishing 2000, 2003
<u>World Book Encyclopedia</u> Vol. 3 copyright © 1974 by Field Enterprises Educational Corp.

Originally published in 2005 by MK Publishing, St. Cloud, Minnesota, USA; (Library of Congress Catalogue Number: 2004118079; ISBN: 0-9763271-0-4)

ISBN: 9781612158204

xulon
PRESS

A Camel's Story: A Search for the Messiah / by Sandy Hanson
Illustrated by Kristi Delage and Sandy Hanson
Graphic Design by Patty K. Haukos
Manufactured in the United States of America

Sandy Hanson welcomes comments and inquiries camelstory@wat.midco.net
Visit the author's website @ www.camelstory.com

This book is available at quality bookstores (Ingram / Spring Arbor Distributors) or online www.xulonpress.com

Prologue

A Search for the Messiah is a picture story for all ages. It is the first book in A Camel's Story Trilogy. All three books are written and produced with love for my family and friends to enjoy for generations to come. May you each find the Messiah for yourself and know how precious you are to Him.

Life is a journey we've been given the opportunity to travel. It is filled with adventure, problems, and questions. As we travel this road called life, the biggest question we will need to answer for ourselves is, "Who is Jesus Christ?" Is he truly the Messiah (savior of all mankind) as the Bible claims He is?

In, A Search for the Messiah, King Balthasar follows a star for thousands of miles using his most prized racing camel, "Xavier", as a pack animal. He's searching for the promised Messiah and is determined to find him.

Xavier certainly did not share in his master's passion. He was very disturbed and angry about being used as a "common mule". Full of self pity, he grumbles, whines, and complains during the entire journey.

Camels, by nature, are much like us. They tend to be rather prideful, stubborn creatures and do not like to follow commands. They want to do what they want to do – when they want to do it!

You will laugh and cry with Xavier as you relate to his doubts and frustrations during the search as well as the dilemma he faces at the journey's end.

May God bless each and every one who reads this story!

Sandy Hanson

HELLO!

MY NAME IS XAVIER BEN HAVEN.

I AM a DROMEDARY CAMEL
from the Middle East!

I HAVE TRAVELED THOUSANDS of MILES
TO TELL YOU MY STORY.

Please, allow me.

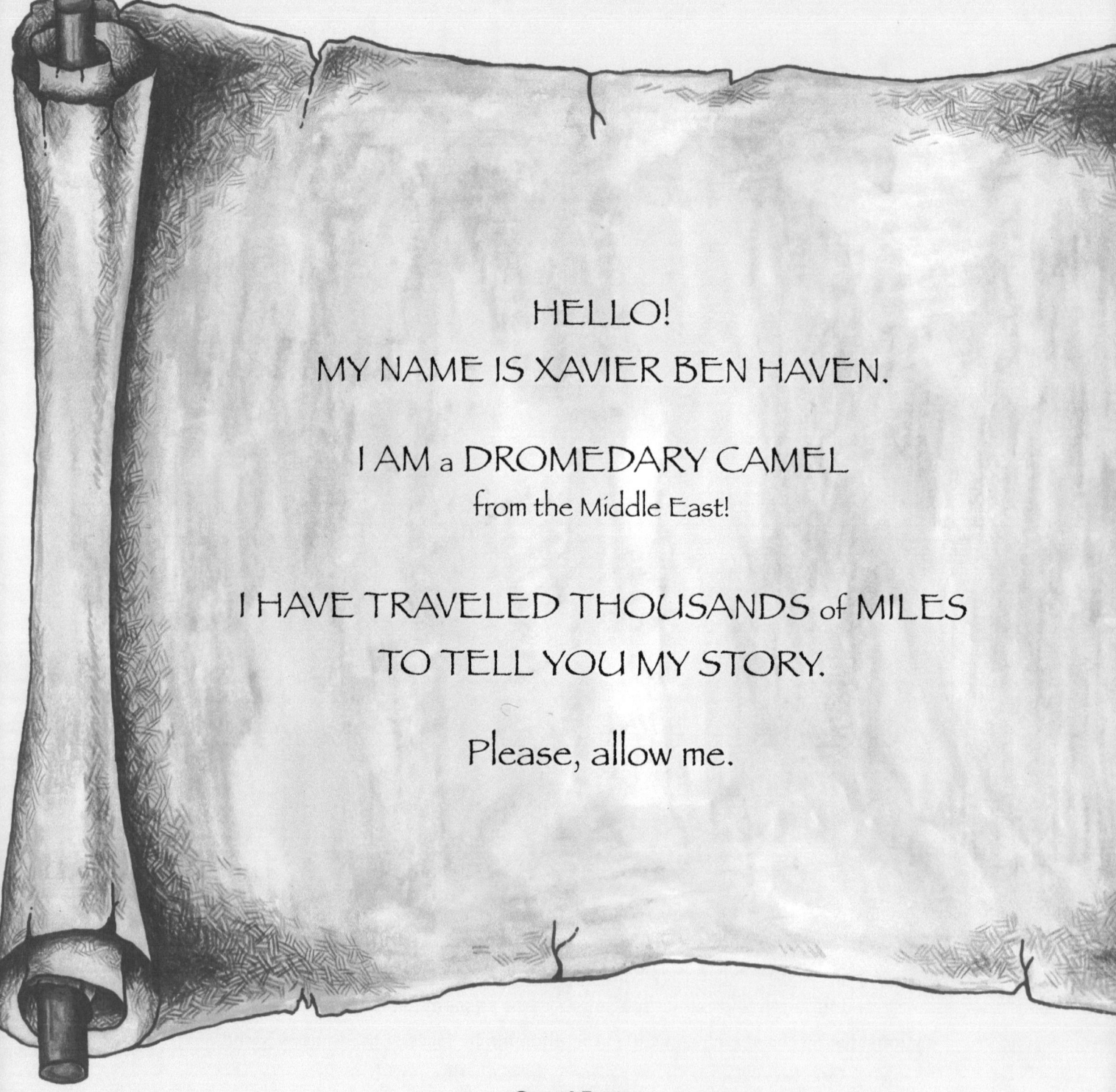

Camel Facts

Camels are the biggest desert mammals – they can live in extremely dry conditions, traveling hundreds of miles across hot, dry deserts with little food or water.

A camel's body stands from 6 to 7 feet tall at the shoulders and it weighs over 1,000 lbs.

The two chief kinds of camels are:
Arabian - which have one hump and live mainly in the Sahara Desert and the Middle East.
Bactrian - which have two humps and live in central Asia.

Hello, I'm XAVIER

It all began many, many years ago on a cold winter's night.
On that night my master, King Balthasar, had just settled me
in my own private quarters at the palace stable.

MINE WAS a VERY COMFORTABLE
and LUXURIOUS STALL.
I HAD EARNED THAT PLACE
because I was the finest of all the king's camels.

After all, I had won him many golden cups at the royal palace races.
I was, indeed, the swiftest camel in the king's fleet

and very proud of my accomplishments
as well as my numerous trophies.

Camel Facts

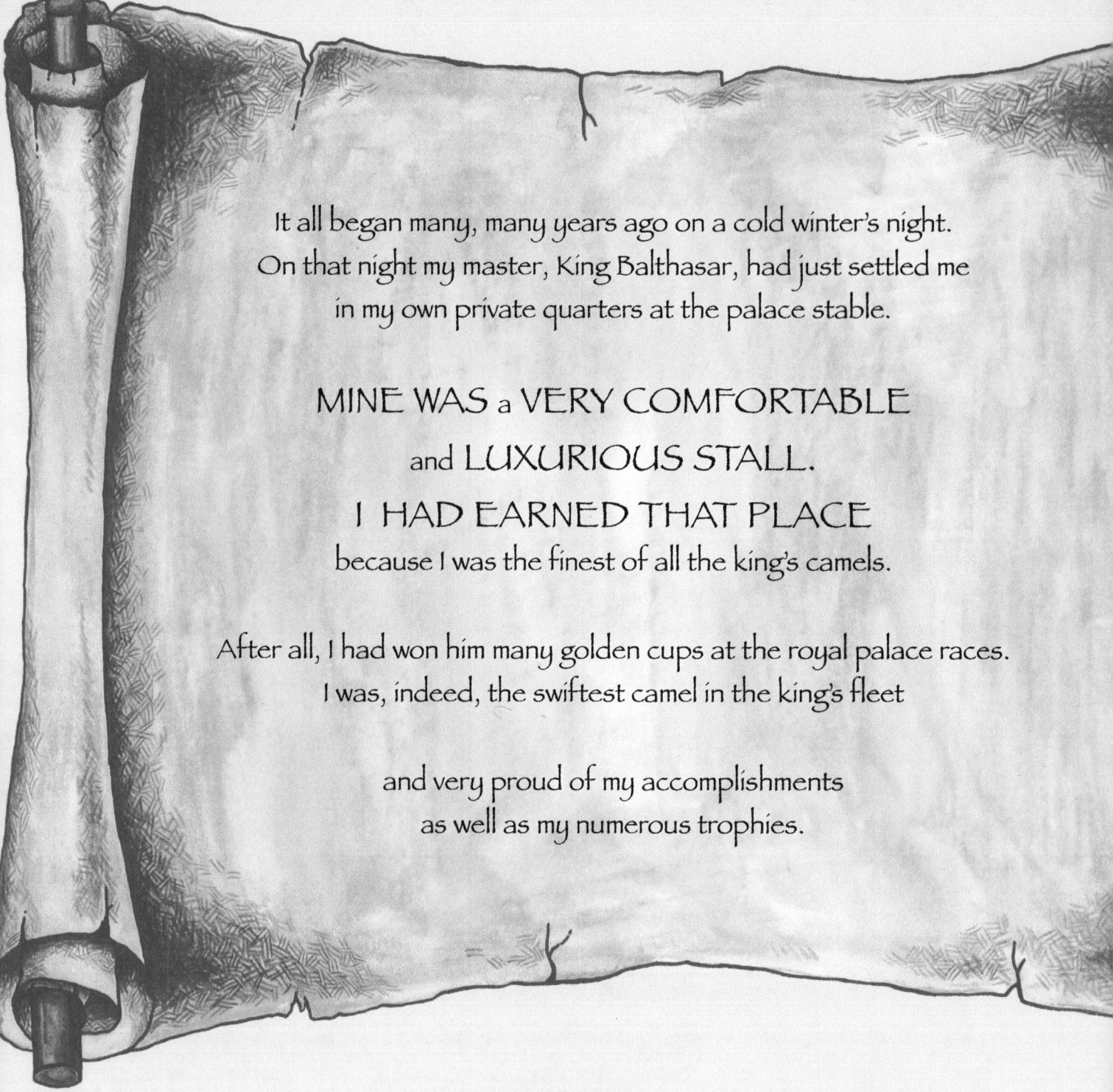

A camel will live to be 17 to 50 years old.

The Arabian camel has been the *ship of the desert*, transporting people and baggage for thousands of years.

A **dromedary camel** is a special kind of Arabian camel raised for riding and racing.

MY STALL WAS COMFORTABLE

MY MASTER WAS VERY PROUD of ME
and treated me with high honor – he made sure
I WAS GIVEN METICULOUS CARE.

I was fed snacks of the most exquisite carrots prior to each race.
His servants kept me fully groomed and bathed at all times, therefore,

I WAS NOT

SMELLY LIKE THE COMMON CAMELS!

I LOVED MY LIFE
and my special treatment!

Camel Facts

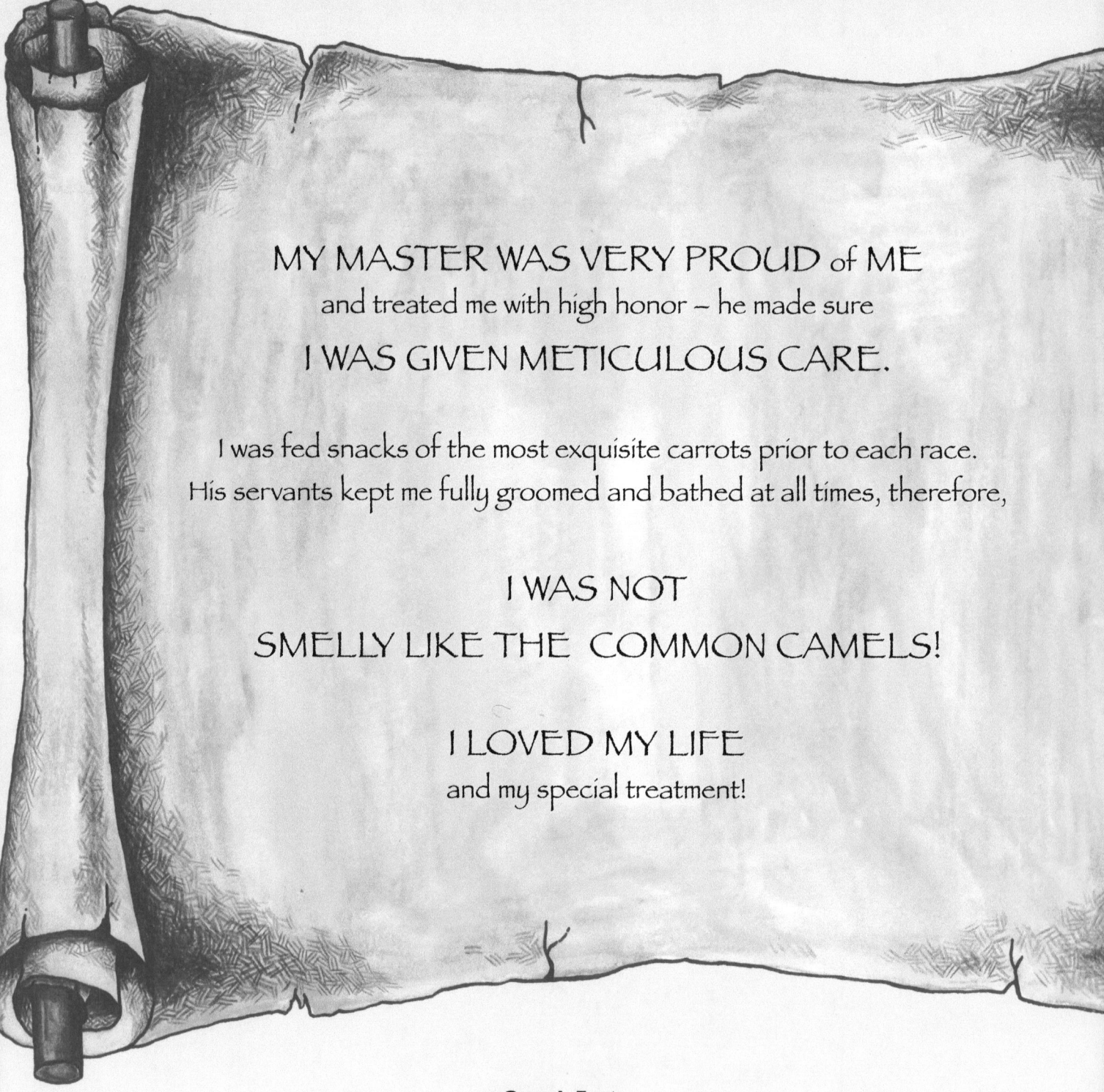

Camels seem larger than they are because of their thick, woolly fur, which may be brown or gray.

Camels have by far the worst smelling breath in the entire animal kingdom.

A camel holds its head high and peers out from under its eyebrows, giving the animal a proud appearance.

Xavier was very proud of all his accomplishments and thought he was better than the rest of the king's camels.

LIFE WAS GRAND

Then one evening,
IT ALL CHANGED in an INSTANT!

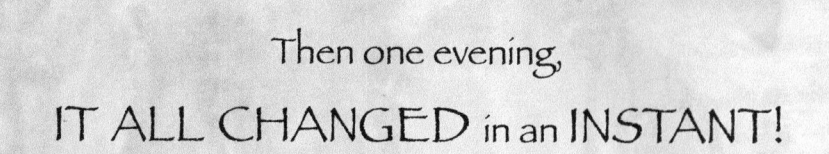

After indulging in my favorite supper, I was sleeping quite comfortably in my plush, well kept quarters. Suddenly I was awakened by my master's voice!
He was commanding me,

"AWAKE, XAVIER! ... AWAKE!

We've no time to lose! We must go now!! HURRY!"

HE KEPT MUMBLING SOMETHING ABOUT a STAR
(the "Star of Bethlehem" as I recall).
Well, at that hour of the night I couldn't have cared less about any old star! I just wanted the royal sleep that was due me!

Camel Facts

Camels do not like to take orders!

They would rather do what they want when they want to do it!

Xavier is a lot like us!

When we are comfortable, we don't like to change — sometimes it's hard for us to take orders.

Y-A-W-N-

I NEED MY SLEEP!

But, no!

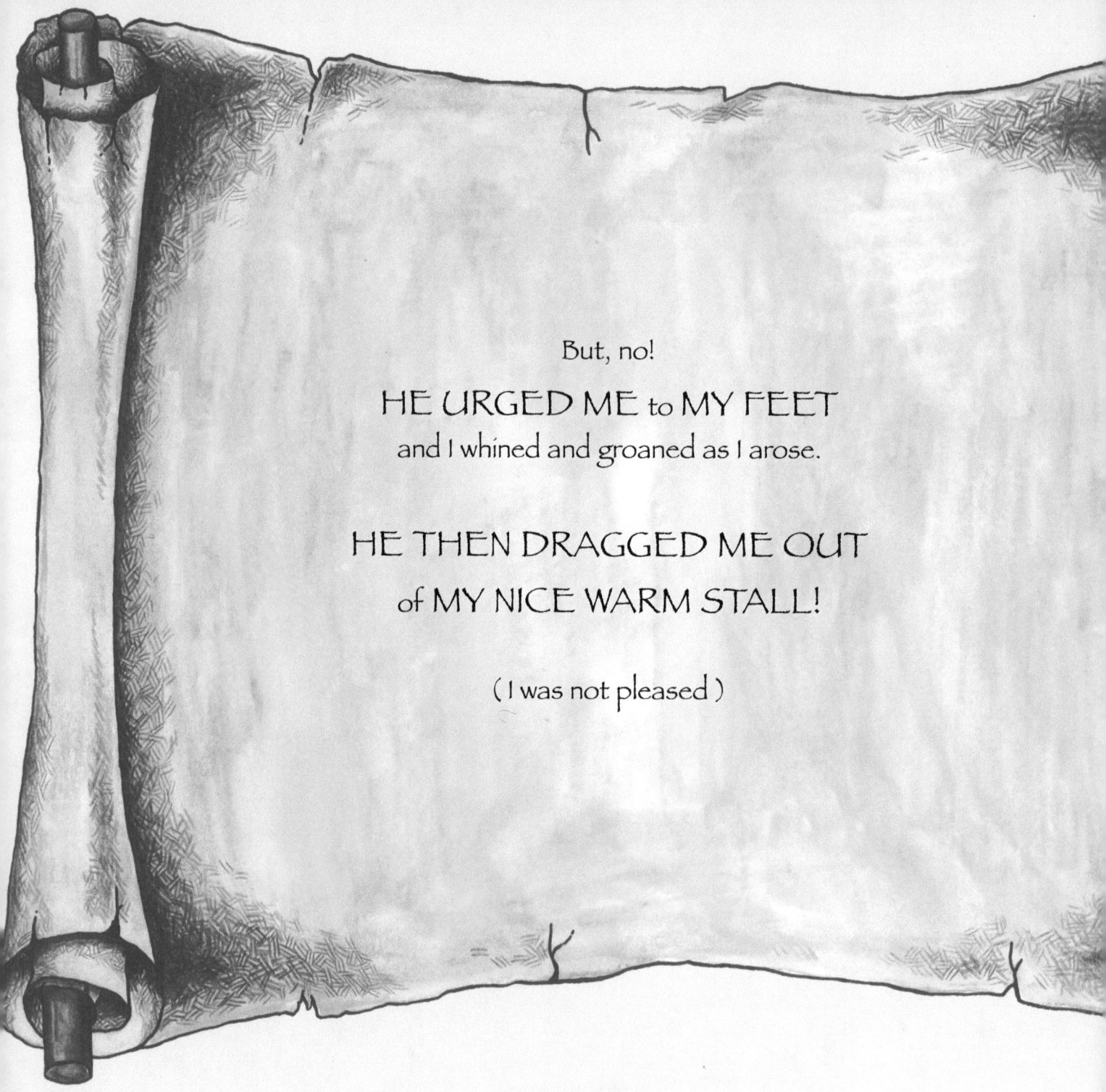

HE URGED ME to MY FEET
and I whined and groaned as I arose.

HE THEN DRAGGED ME OUT
of MY NICE WARM STALL!

(I was not pleased)

More Camel Facts

Camels never learn to obey man freely as do horses, dogs, and some other animals.

They are rather stubborn creatures.

Have you ever been stubborn?

HE
DRAGGED ME OUT
of MY STALL

Balthasar led me to a near by storage area that held supplies of all sorts. There were packs of food, cooking utensils, and blankets — I suspect he'd been packing for quite some time.

Then, to my astonishment — HE BEGAN LOADING THESE PACKAGES onto MY BACK! I protested, thinking, "I AM NOT a BEAST of BURDEN"!

Surely you cannot expect a camel of my position and status to perform such a menial task?

WHAT YOU NEED is a DONKEY
. . . Yes — a common mule!"

Camel Facts

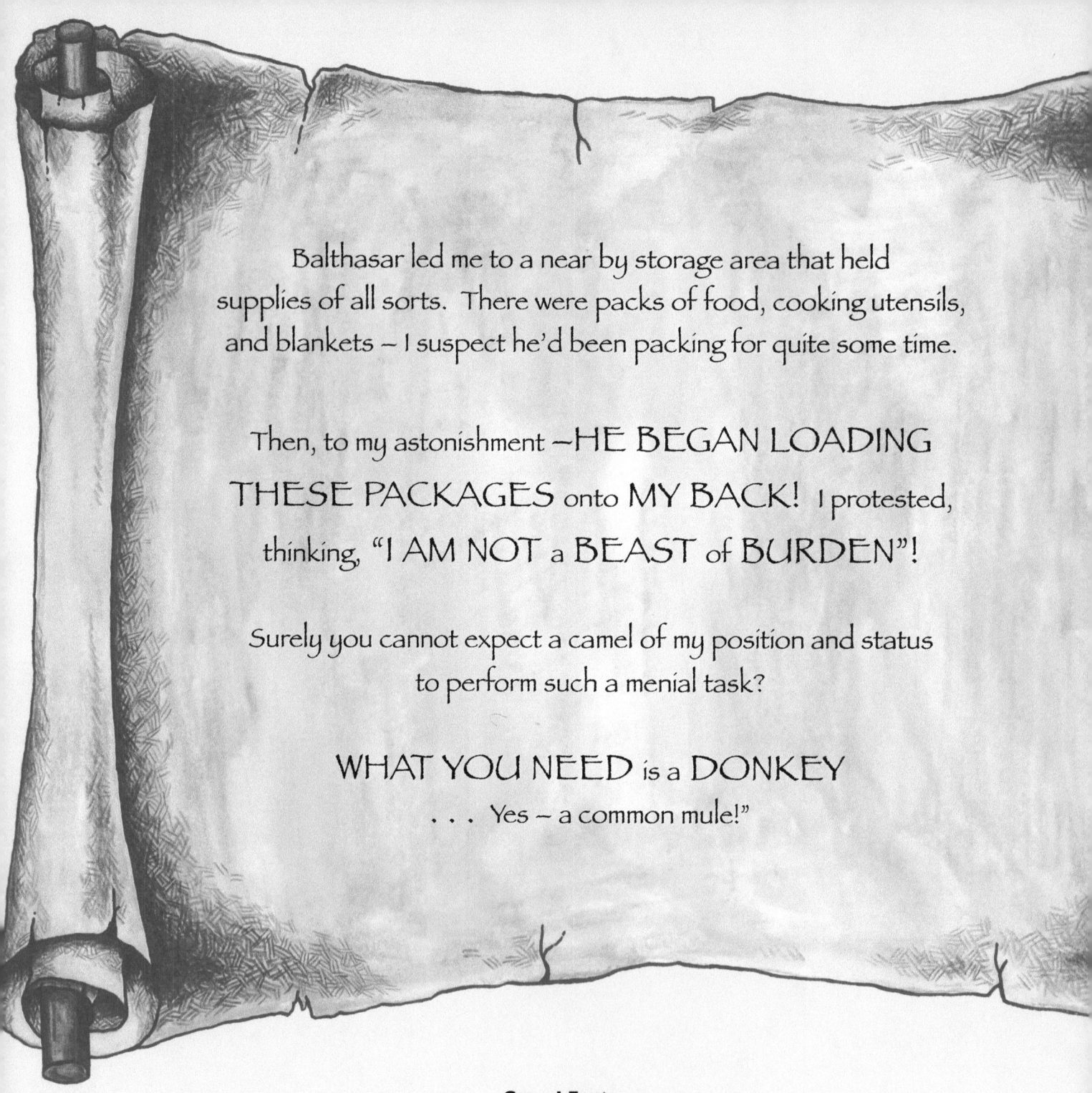

A camel whines when anyone mounts it or puts a pack on its back, then it grunts and groans loudly as it rises to its feet.

The camel is easily annoyed, and will spit at anything nearby.

Xavier thought he was too good to be used for a pack animal — racing was for him! This job, he thought, was for somebody less important than he was.

Xavier was full of false pride.

I AM NOT
A
BEAST OF BURDEN!

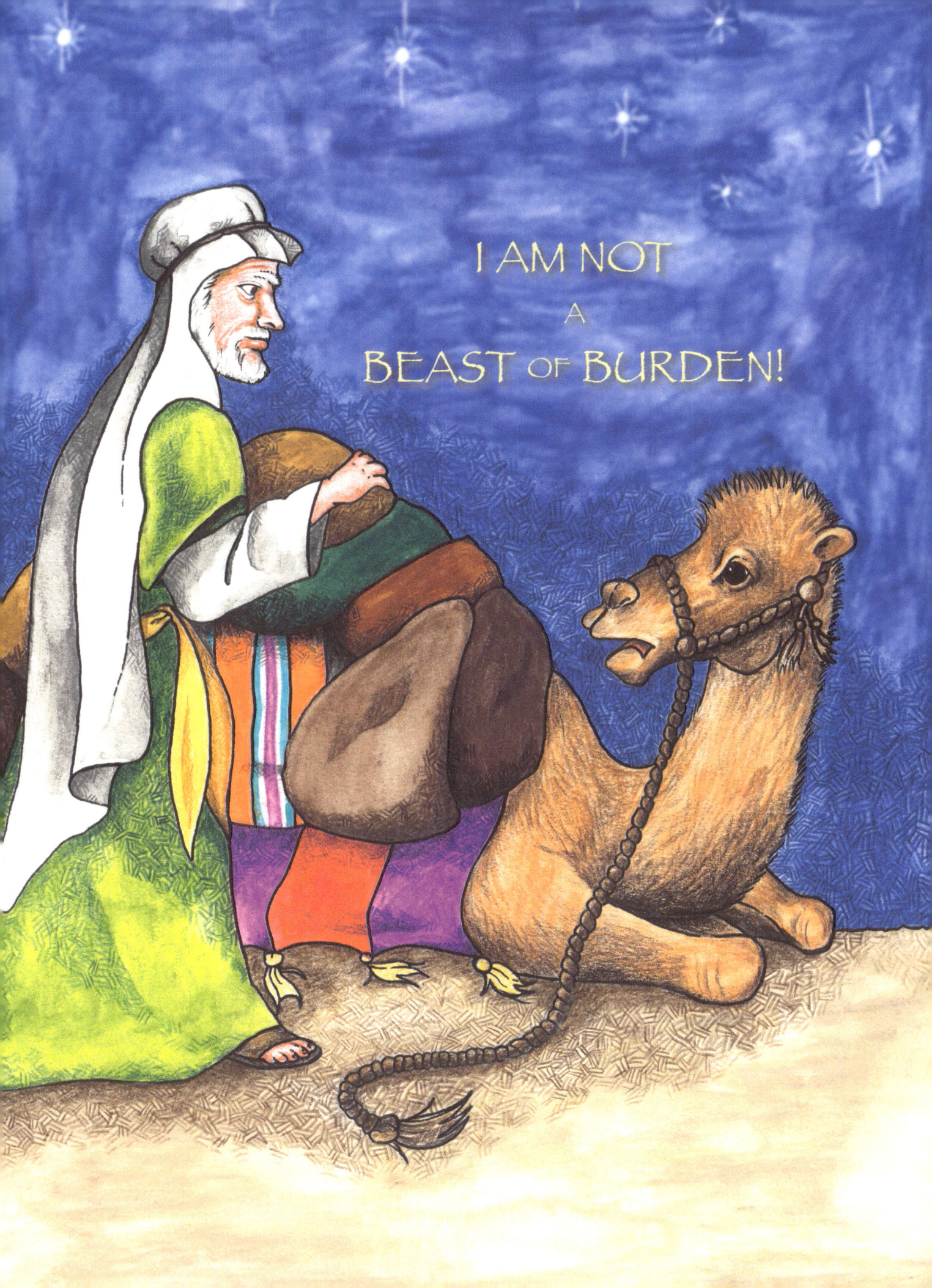

He ignored my resistance and continued to load me
with the disgusting burdens. I was appalled, wondering...
"What did I do to deserve such disgrace and humiliation?"

I DIDN'T GIVE a "CAMEL'S WHINE" ABOUT any OLD STAR!

He hurried me on the path and kept pointing to the star.
He led me, but I followed along unwillingly.
I couldn't believe he would treat me this way,
after all, I had been his most prized camel!

I WAS BORN for NOBILITY!

To be ridden by kings –
and for racing – never to be a mere beast of burden!

Camel Facts

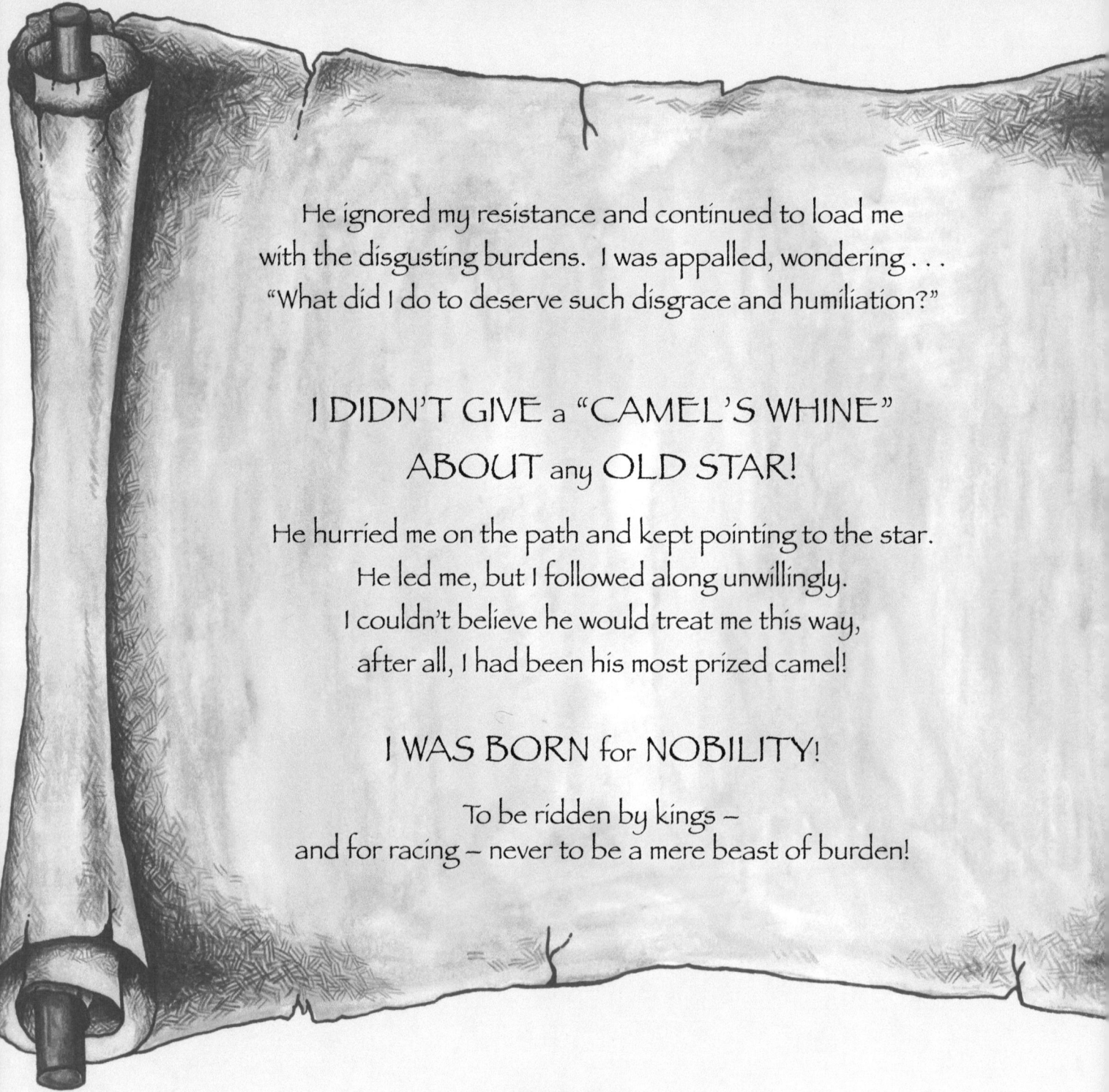

Dromedary camels are usually not used to carry heavy packs,
but are used for riding and racing because they are faster than other Arabian camels.

The Arabian camels, normally used for transporting goods, can carry as much as 1,000 lbs. –
but they move as slowly as 2 ½ miles per hour enabling them to travel only about 25 miles per day.

Dromedaries can travel as far as 100 miles per day and can run at speeds of about 10 miles per hour.

I DIDN'T GIVE A CAMEL'S WHINE ABOUT ANY OLD STAR!

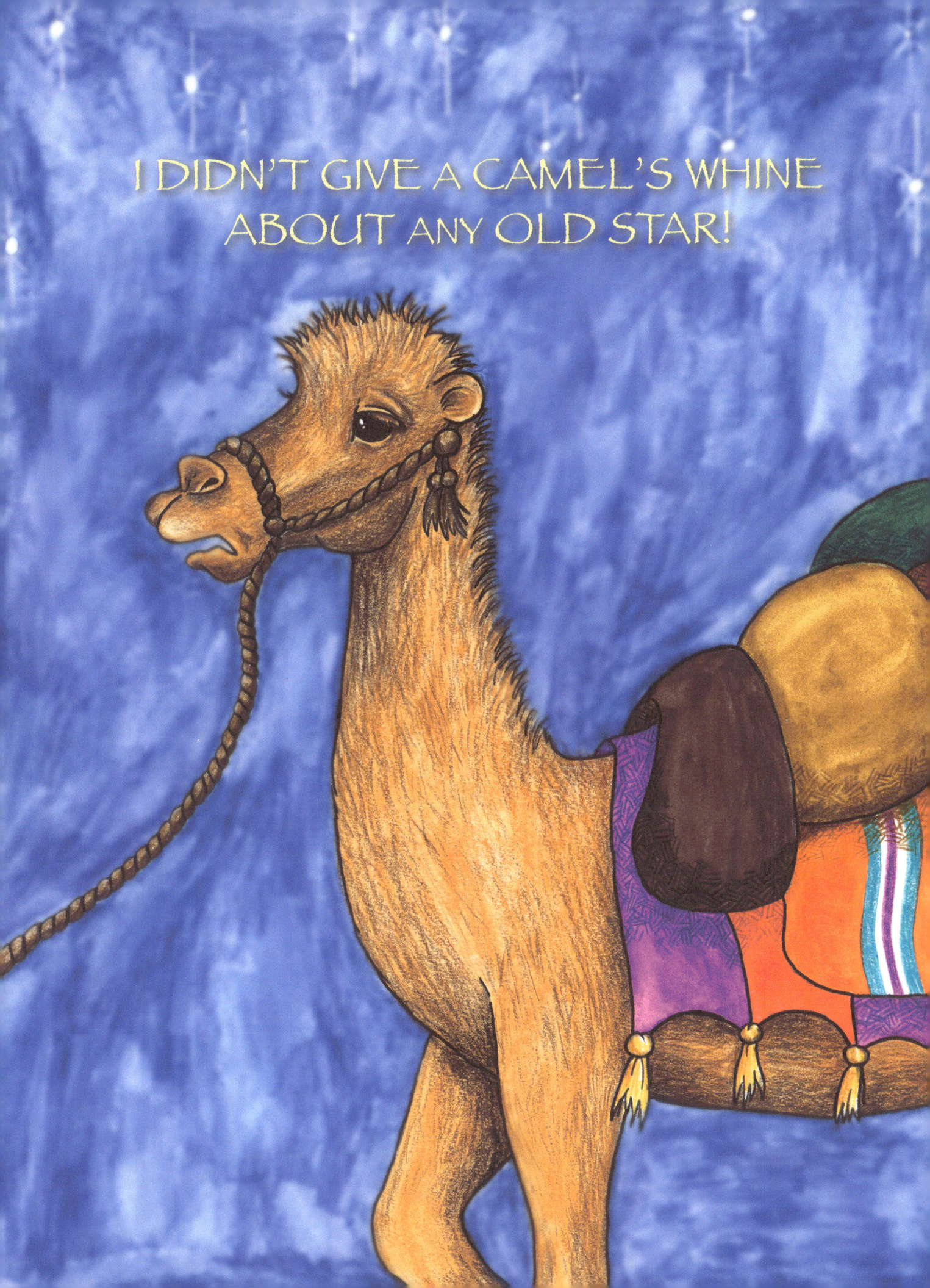

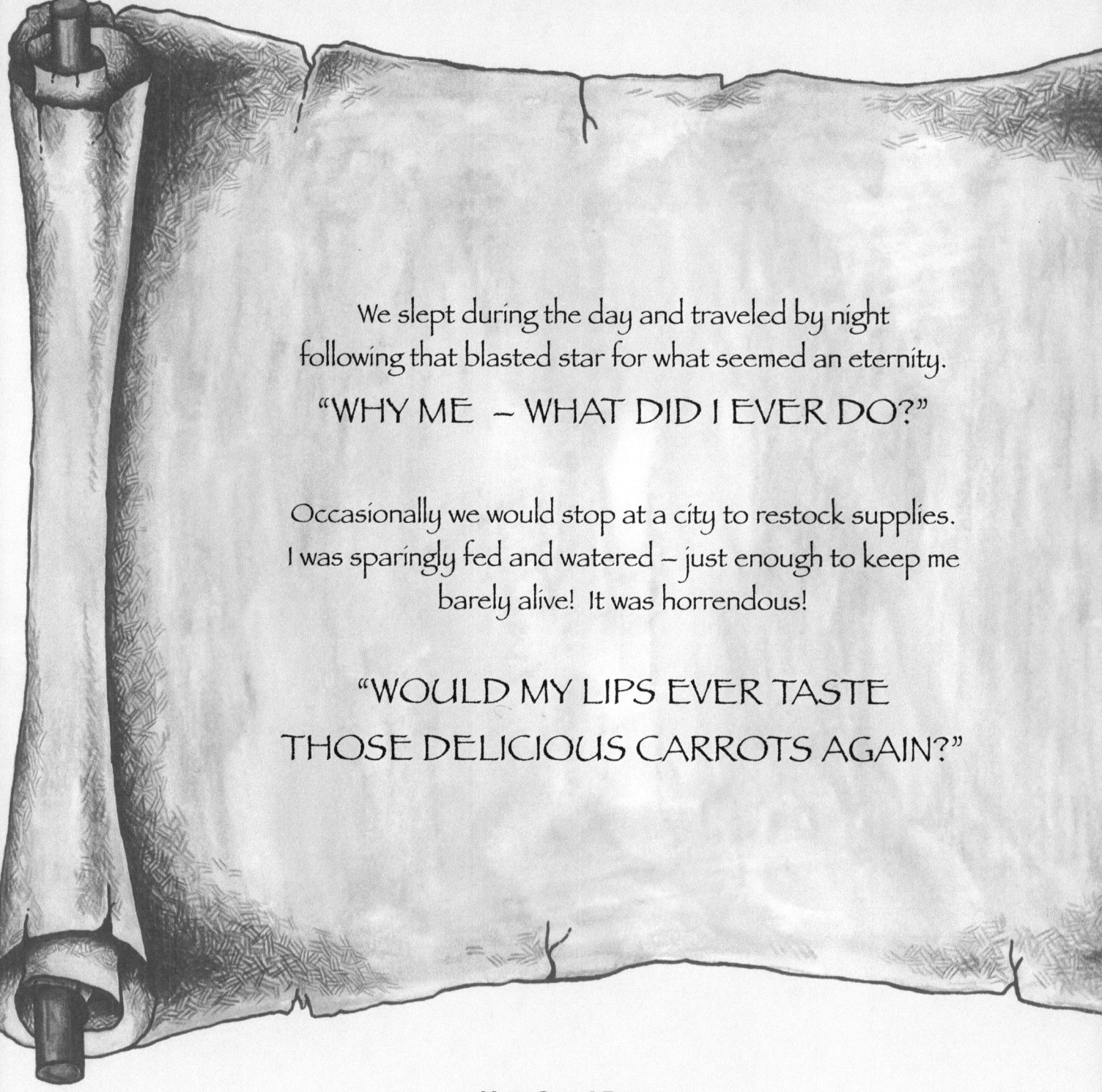

We slept during the day and traveled by night
following that blasted star for what seemed an eternity.
"WHY ME – WHAT DID I EVER DO?"

Occasionally we would stop at a city to restock supplies.
I was sparingly fed and watered – just enough to keep me
barely alive! It was horrendous!

"WOULD MY LIPS EVER TASTE
THOSE DELICIOUS CARROTS AGAIN?"

More Camel Facts

A camel carries its own built-in food supply in the form of a hump.

A camel's hump is made of fat, but the camel's body can break the fat down into food and water when these are scarce.

Camels can go many days or even months without water. But when water is available,
they can drink over 50 gallons in a day.

The camel's feet have two joined toes to stop them from sinking into soft sand. The camel's nostrils can close up
completely to block out blowing sand.

Camels have a double row of eyelashes to protect their eyes from sand and sun.

WHY ME?

FINALLY,

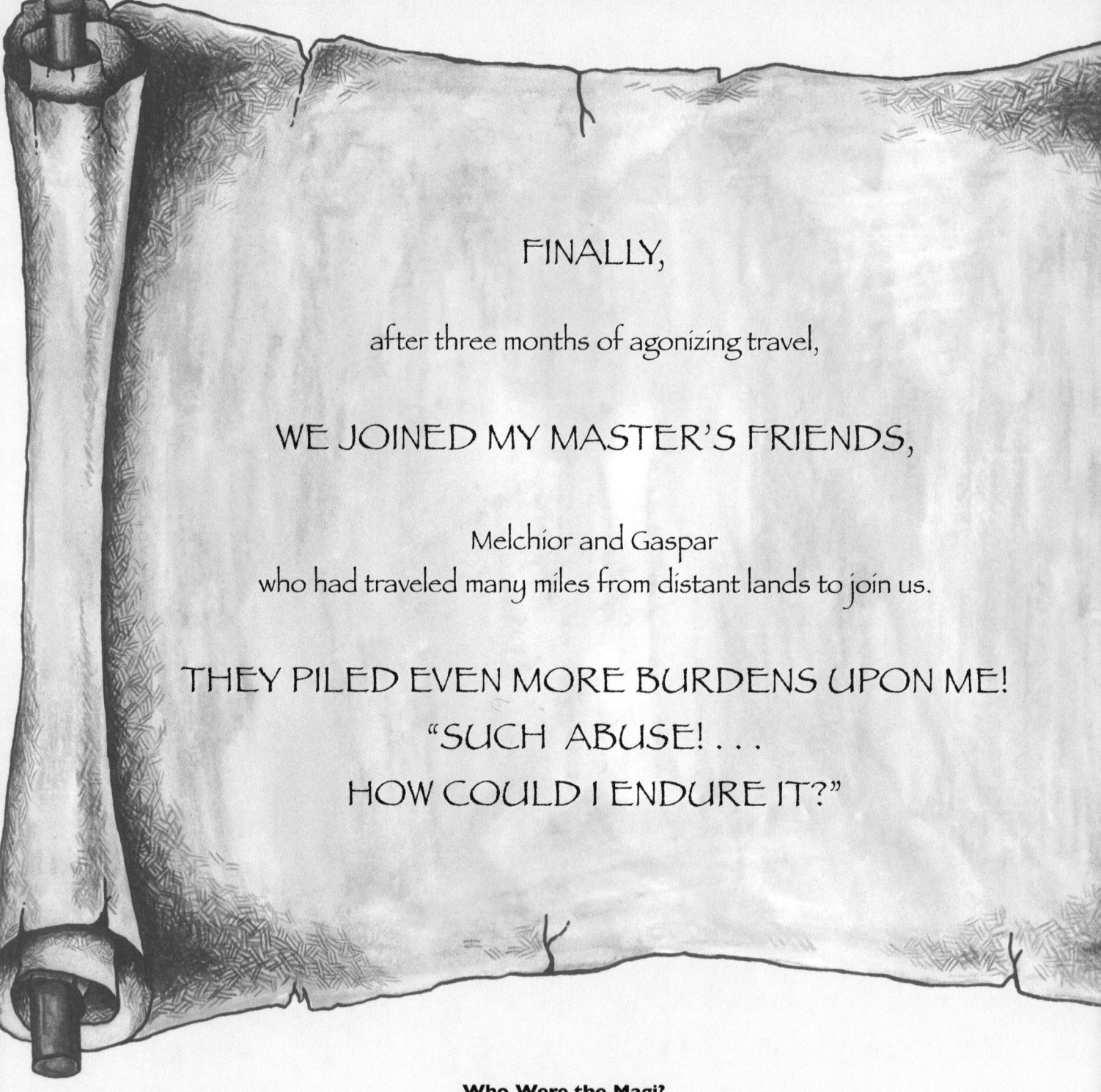

after three months of agonizing travel,

WE JOINED MY MASTER'S FRIENDS,

Melchior and Gaspar
who had traveled many miles from distant lands to join us.

THEY PILED EVEN MORE BURDENS UPON ME!
"SUCH ABUSE! . . .
HOW COULD I ENDURE IT?"

Who Were the Magi?

Not much is known about these Magi (traditionally called wisemen).

Tradition says they were men of high position from Parthia, near the site of ancient Babylon.

We're not sure how many there were, but these men from far away lands recognized Jesus as the Messiah when most of God's chosen people in Israel did not.

They traveled thousands of miles to see him.

The Bible Says
Magi from the east came to Jerusalem and asked, "Where is the one who has been born King of the Jews? We saw his star in the east and have come to worship him." *(Matthew 2: 1-2)*

WHAT A DISGRACE!

WE CONTINUED
THIS WAY for THOUSANDS
of MILES.

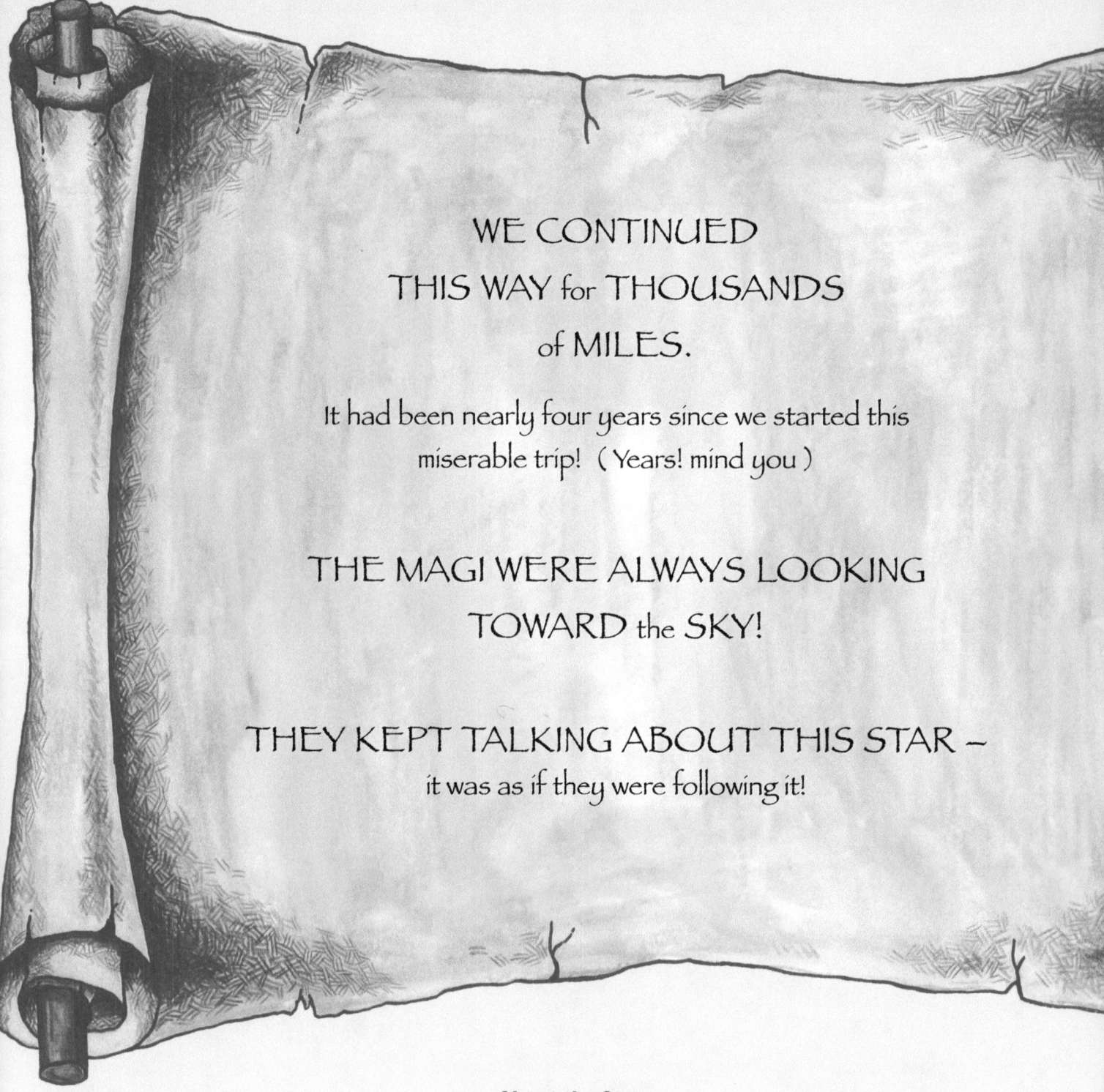

It had been nearly four years since we started this miserable trip! (Years! mind you)

THE MAGI WERE ALWAYS LOOKING
TOWARD the SKY!

THEY KEPT TALKING ABOUT THIS STAR –
it was as if they were following it!

About the Star

The magi said they saw his star in the east -- Balaam referred to a coming "star ... out of Jacob" *(Numbers 24: 17)*.

"Some say this star may have been a conjunction of Jupiter, Saturn, and Mars in 6 B.C. and others offer other explanations. But if God created the heavens and the earth as the Bible says He did, in Genesis, couldn't He have created a special star to signal the arrival of his Son?"

"Whatever the nature of the star, the wisemen followed it!"

THEY KEPT TALKING ABOUT THIS STAR

Then one day, my master spoke to me. He said,
"Xavier, thank you for being so patient."

(If only he'd known how angry I was at having been
forced to come on this expedition!)

I WAS SO MAD I COULD HAVE SPIT!

He continued, "We are almost there, faithful one!
I knew you were the only one of all my camels who would have
the strength and stamina to carry such a heavy load on this long
journey. Yes, you're the only one who could have endured it."

I THOUGHT to MYSELF ANGRILY, "YES, and I'M NEARLY DEAD – I HOPE YOU'RE HAPPY!"

A Camel with a Bad Attitude?

Xavier's master, Balthasar, was very thankful for his fine young camel
and he even thanked Xavier for being so patient.

Balthasar could not tell from looking at his camel's
outward appearance how much anger and self pity filled Xavier's heart.

The Bible says only God knows what is in our hearts. *(2 Chronicles 6: 30; 1 Kings 8:39; Luke 16: 15)*

"The Lord does not look at the things man looks at. Man looks at the outward appearance,
but the Lord looks at the heart." *(1 Samuel 16: 7)*

I WAS SO MAD

I COULD HAVE SPIT!

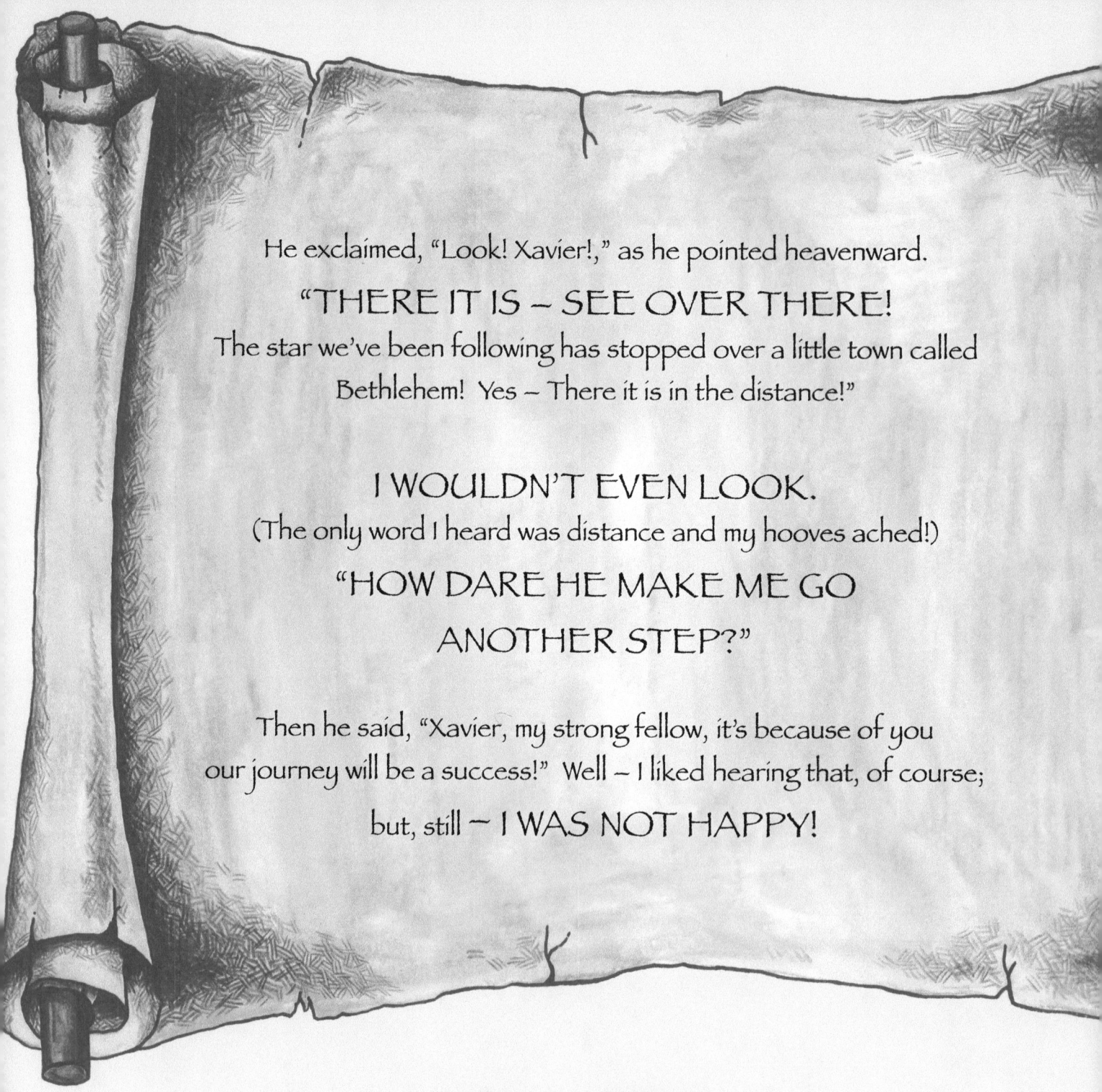

He exclaimed, "Look! Xavier!," as he pointed heavenward.

"THERE IT IS – SEE OVER THERE!
The star we've been following has stopped over a little town called
Bethlehem! Yes – There it is in the distance!"

I WOULDN'T EVEN LOOK.
(The only word I heard was distance and my hooves ached!)

"HOW DARE HE MAKE ME GO ANOTHER STEP?"

Then he said, "Xavier, my strong fellow, it's because of you
our journey will be a success!" Well – I liked hearing that, of course;
but, still – I WAS NOT HAPPY!

Was Xavier Being Stubborn?

Xavier was so focused on himself and his own misery that he didn't want to think about anything else.
Even though Xavier's master was trying to include him in the search and let him share in the whole experience,
Xavier refused to be a part of it because his heart was not open.

The Bible says "Today, if you hear his voice, do not harden your hearts." *(Psalm 95: 7-8)*

Don't let your heart be stubborn like Xavier's!

I WOULDN'T EVEN LOOK!

He then declared, "It's because of you

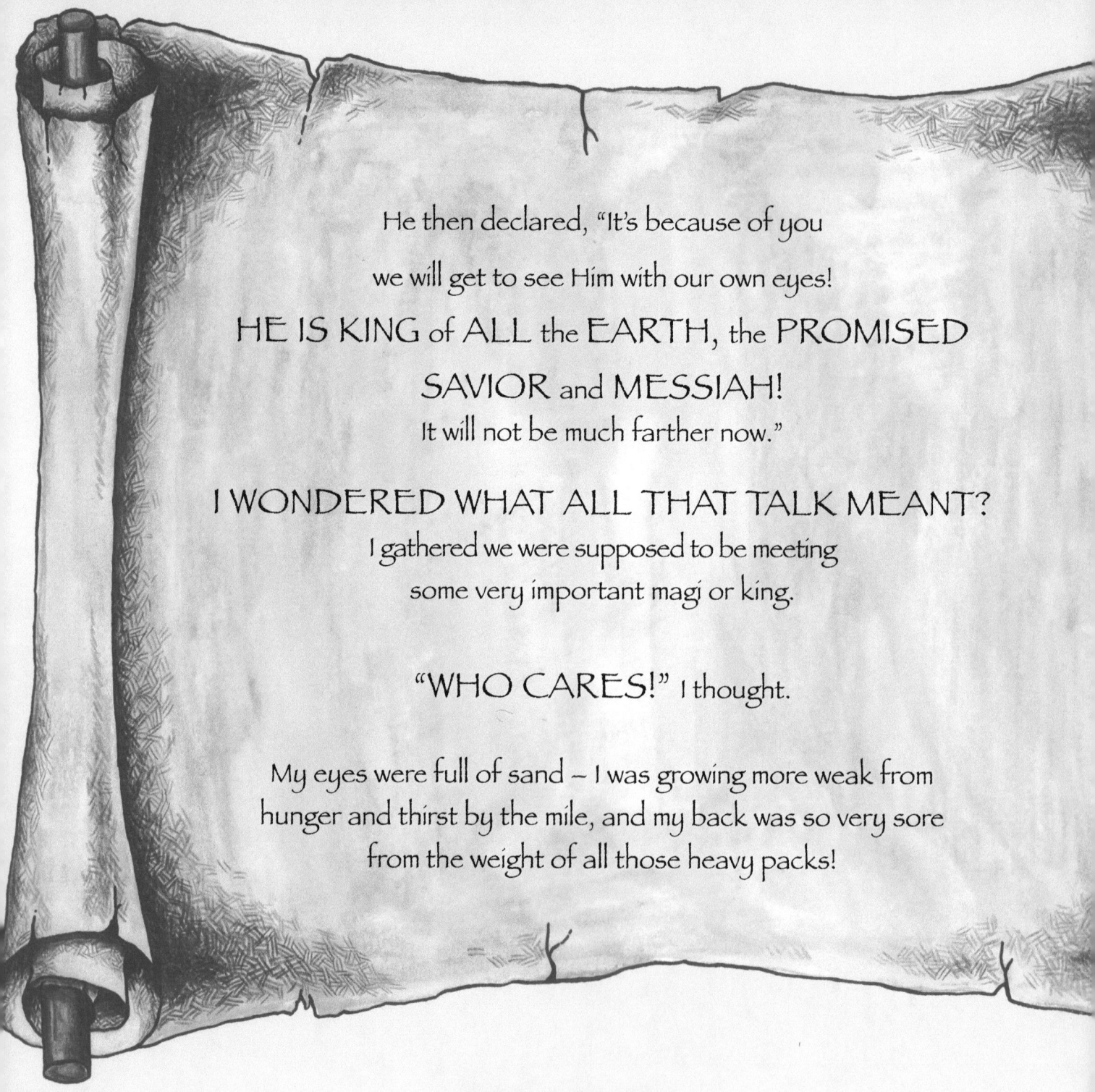

we will get to see Him with our own eyes!

HE IS KING of ALL the EARTH, the PROMISED

SAVIOR and MESSIAH!

It will not be much farther now."

I WONDERED WHAT ALL THAT TALK MEANT?
I gathered we were supposed to be meeting
some very important magi or king.

"WHO CARES!" I thought.

My eyes were full of sand – I was growing more weak from
hunger and thirst by the mile, and my back was so very sore
from the weight of all those heavy packs!

Was the Camel Selfish?

Yes! Xavier was so focused on himself that he couldn't even try
to see the bigger picture. He wondered about what he was being told, but only for a moment.

Xavier couldn't share in his master's enthusiasm or try
to understand what he was saying because all he really cared about was himself.

Being self-centered rather than God-centered causes us to be narrow minded and limits us
from becoming who God created us to be.

WHO CARES!

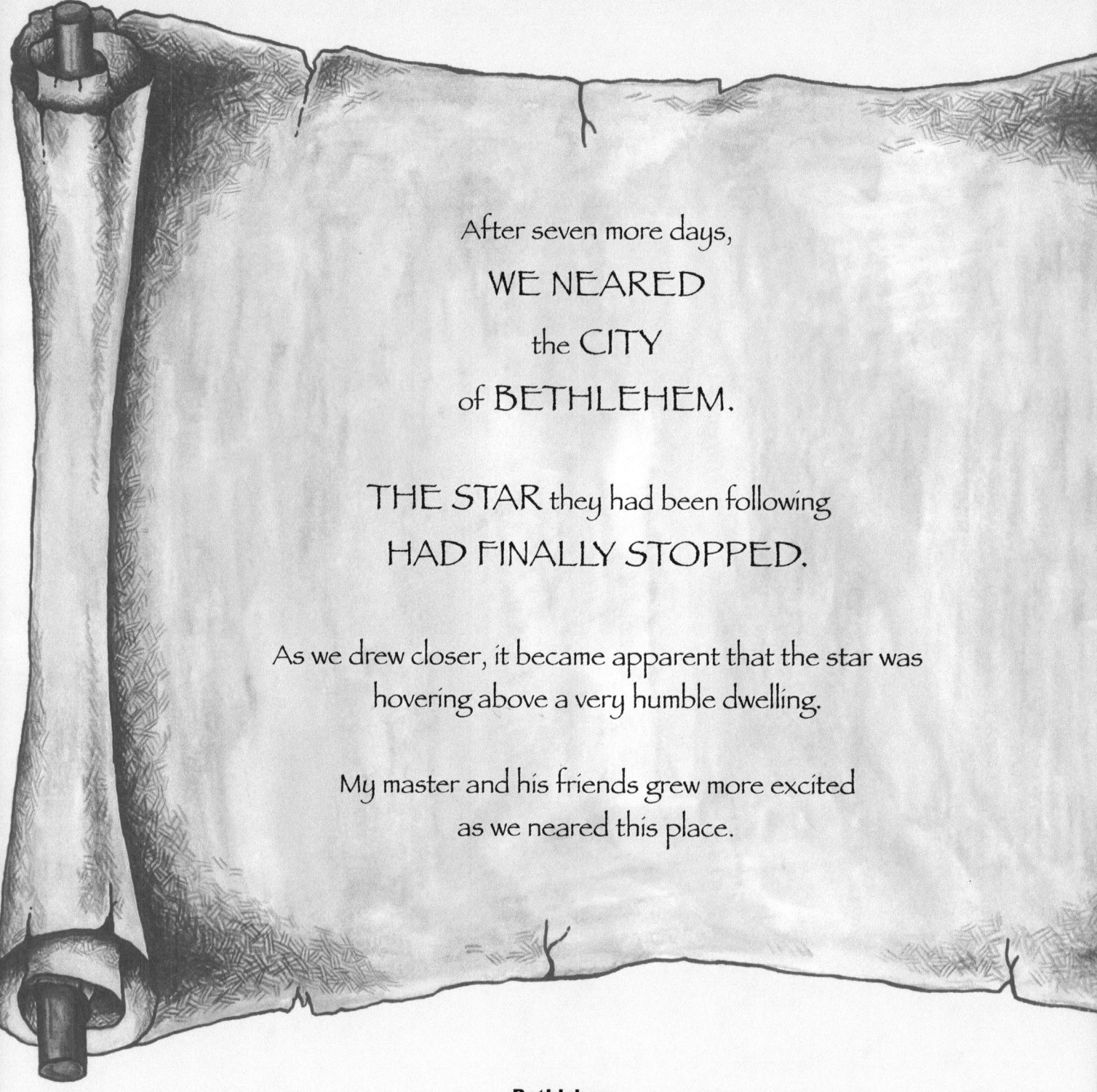

After seven more days,
WE NEARED
the CITY
of BETHLEHEM.

THE STAR they had been following
HAD FINALLY STOPPED.

As we drew closer, it became apparent that the star was hovering above a very humble dwelling.

My master and his friends grew more excited as we neared this place.

Bethlehem

Bethlehem, a town in Jordan, is the birthplace of Jesus Christ. It is a small town, about 5 miles south of Jerusalem, located in the district which was called Ephrathah at the time of Jesus' birth.

The Bible says
"King Herod and the people of Jerusalem were disturbed when they learned that the magi were searching for "the King of the Jews".

The magi knew where he was to be born because it had been foretold. So when King Herod asked them where the child was to be born, they told him: "In Bethlehem in Judea." They replied, "for this is what the prophet has written ..." *(Matthew 2: 5, 6)*

"But you, Bethlehem Ephrathah, though you are small among the clans of Judah, out of you will come for me one who will be ruler over Israel, whose origins are from old, from ancient times." *(Micah 5: 2)*

THE STAR STOPPED AT BETHLEHEM

When we arrived,
my master bid one of his friends to go inside and inquire.
King Gaspar went inside and soon returned rejoicing.

"WE'VE FOUND HIM —
WE'VE FOUND HIM! The MESSIAH!"

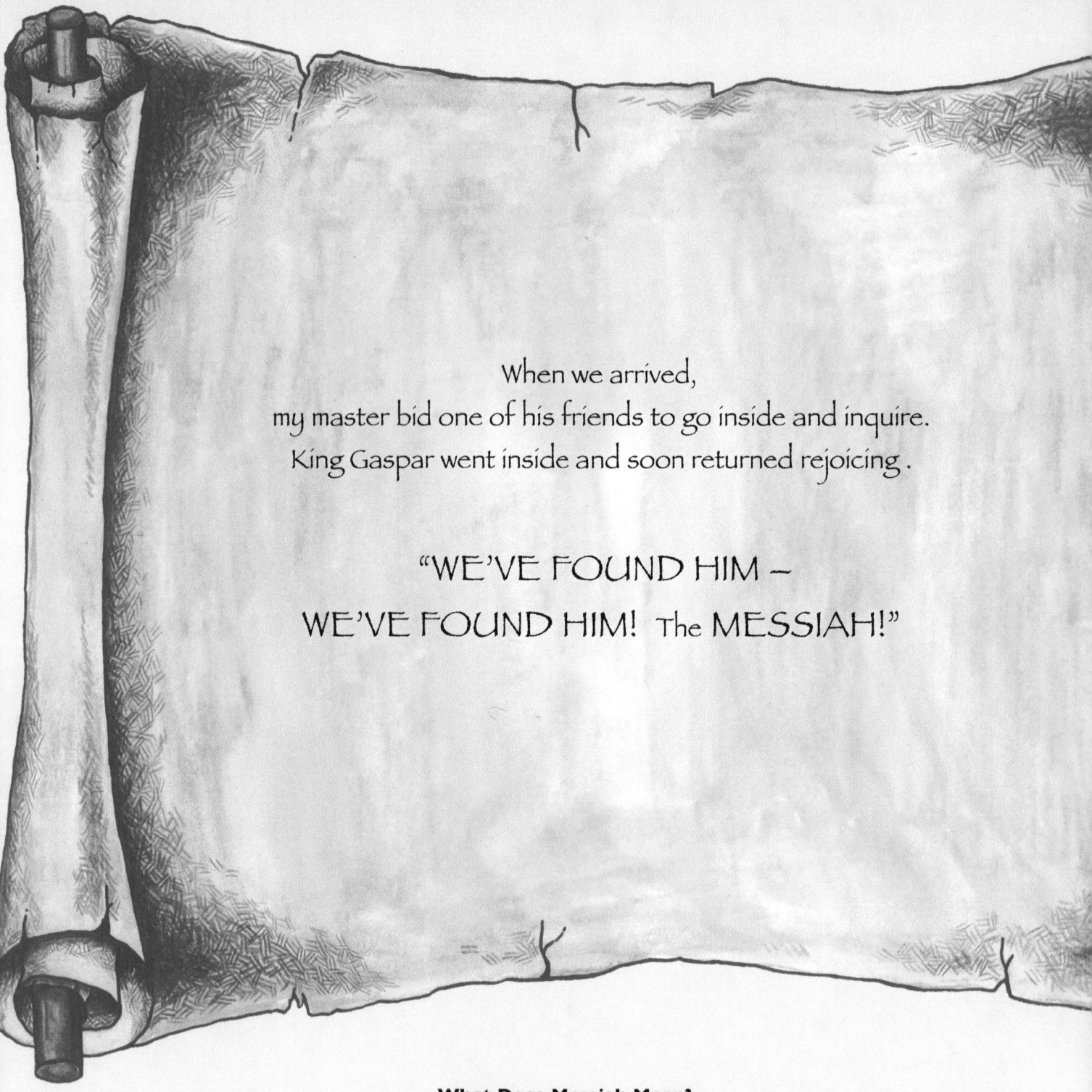

What Does Messiah Mean?

Messiah is a Hebrew word meaning "*the anointed one*". It has the same meaning as the Greek word, *Christos*, or Christ.

The prophets in biblical times spoke of a king who would redeem Israel and bring about a period of peace and justice on earth. They believed that he would be a direct descendant of King David.
The term Messiah came to refer to this ideal king.

The Bible says Jesus was a direct descendant of King David. (see *Matthew 1: 1-17* for record of the birth line of Jesus)
"He will stand and shepherd his flock in the strength of the Lord, in the majesty of the name of the Lord his God and they will live securely, for then his greatness will reach to the ends of the earth and he will be their peace." *(Micah 5: 4, 5)*

The woman at the well spoke to Jesus, "I know the Messiah is coming — when he comes,
he will explain everything to us." Then Jesus declared, "I who speak to you am he." *(John 4: 25, 26)*

29

WE'VE FOUND THE MESSIAH!

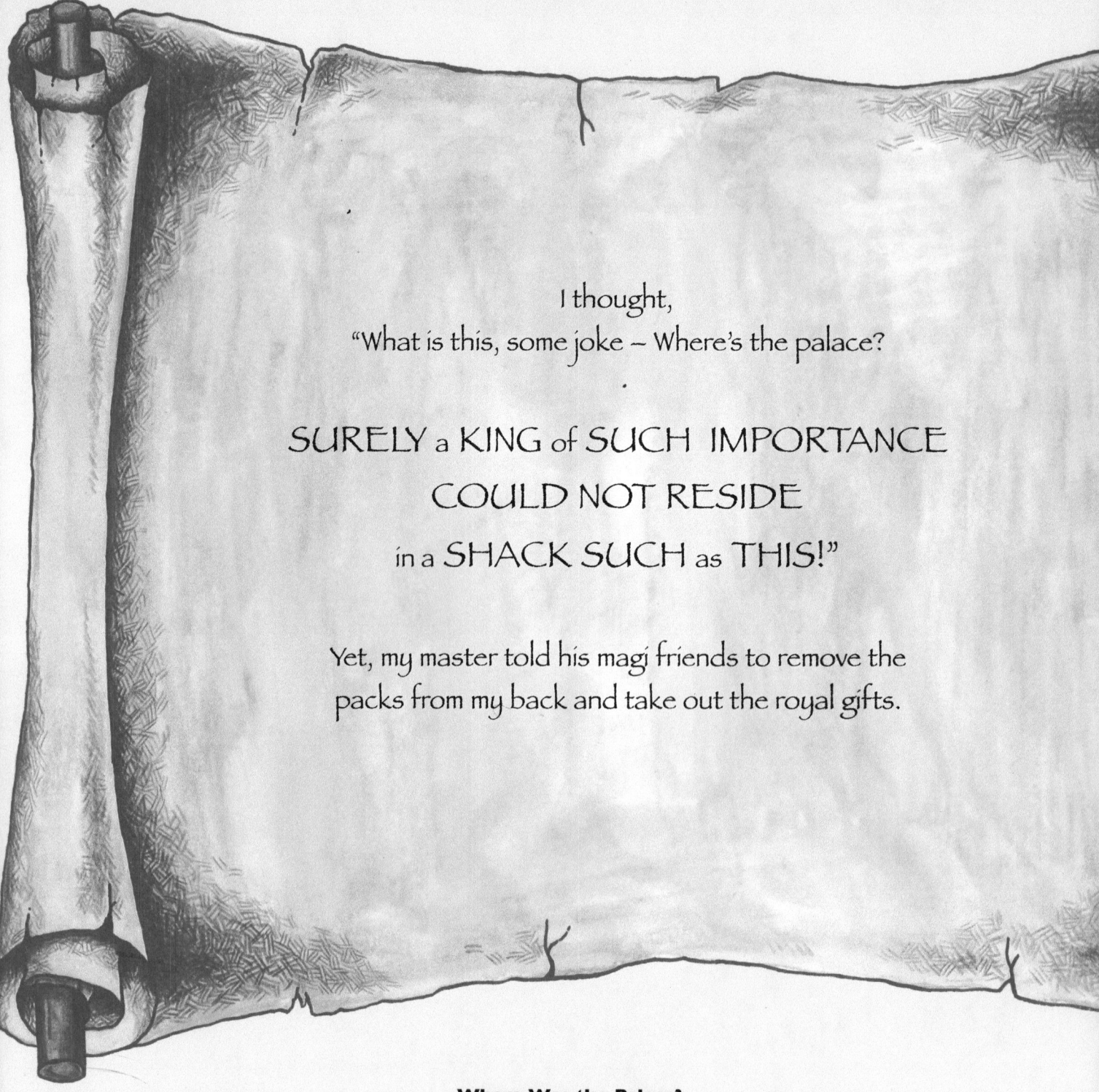

I thought,
"What is this, some joke – Where's the palace?

SURELY a KING of SUCH IMPORTANCE
COULD NOT RESIDE
in a SHACK SUCH as THIS!"

Yet, my master told his magi friends to remove the packs from my back and take out the royal gifts.

Where Was the Palace?

Xavier was not the only one who was expecting the Messiah to be found in a palace.
Jesus was probably 1 or 2 years old when the magi found him.
Many of the Jews, God's own chosen people, were looking for an earthly king and would not recognize Jesus as the Messiah because of his humble birth.

Jesus said "My kingdom is not of this world." *(John 18: 36)*
"When the Son of Man comes in his glory, and all the angels with him, he will sit on his throne in heavenly glory. All the nations will be gathered before him." *(Matthew 25: 31, 32)*
When Jesus comes back, He will come back as King!

WHERE'S THE PALACE?

As the burdens were lifted from me,

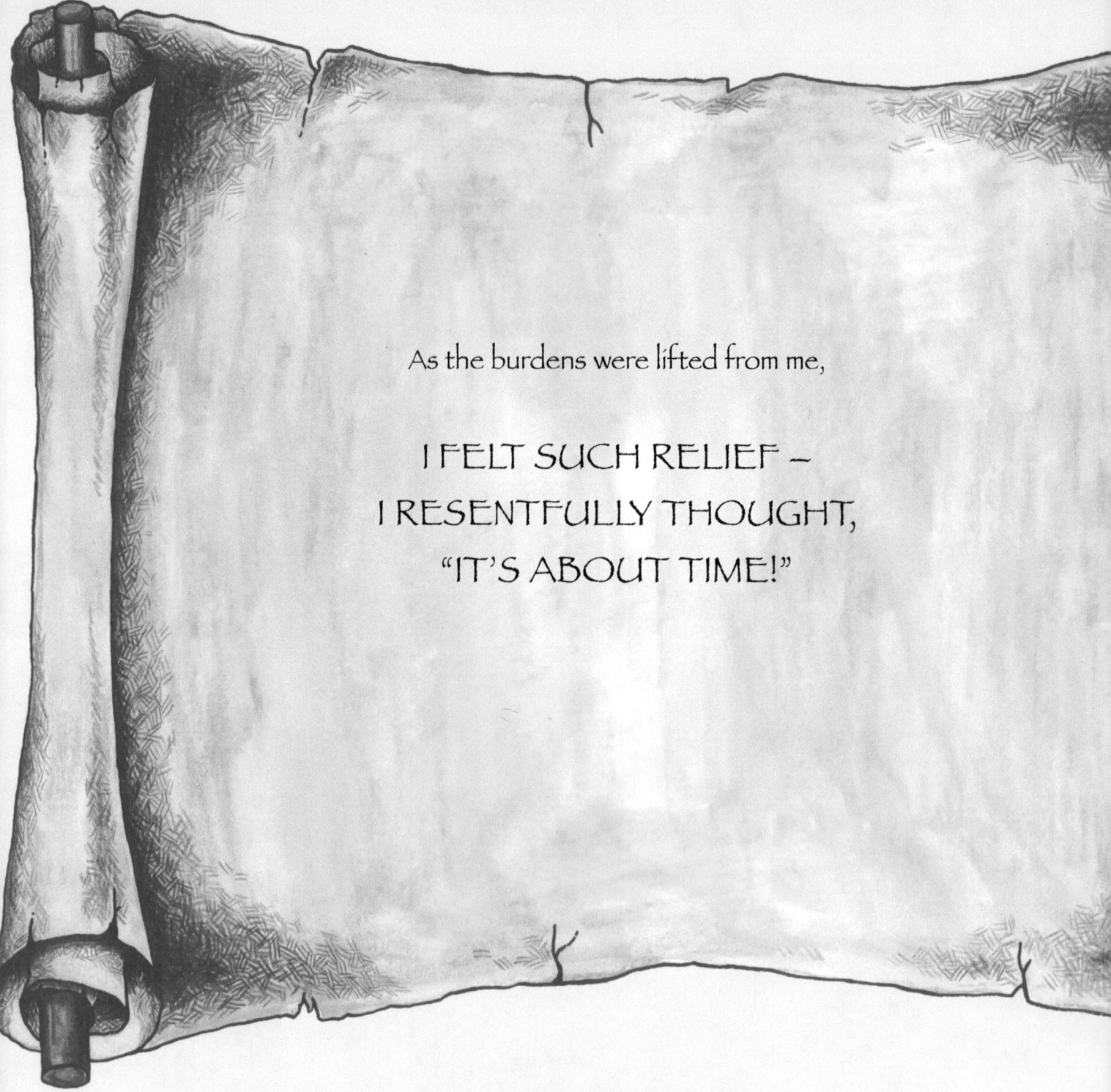

I FELT SUCH RELIEF –
I RESENTFULLY THOUGHT,
"IT'S ABOUT TIME!"

Xavier Was Only Thinking of #1

Xavier was still angry that he'd been forced to come on the search.
He was envious of the other camels because he was the only camel required to carry the packs.
Xavier really did not care about anyone or anything other than his own comfort.

The Bible says, "If any of you lacks wisdom, he should ask God,
who gives generously to all without finding fault; and it will be given to him." *(James 1: 5)*

"Who is wise and understanding among you? Let him show it by his good life, by deeds done in the humility
that comes from wisdom. But, if you harbor bitter envy and selfish ambition in your hearts,
do not boast about it or deny the truth." *(James 3: 13-14)*

Being selfish and self-centered is not wise.

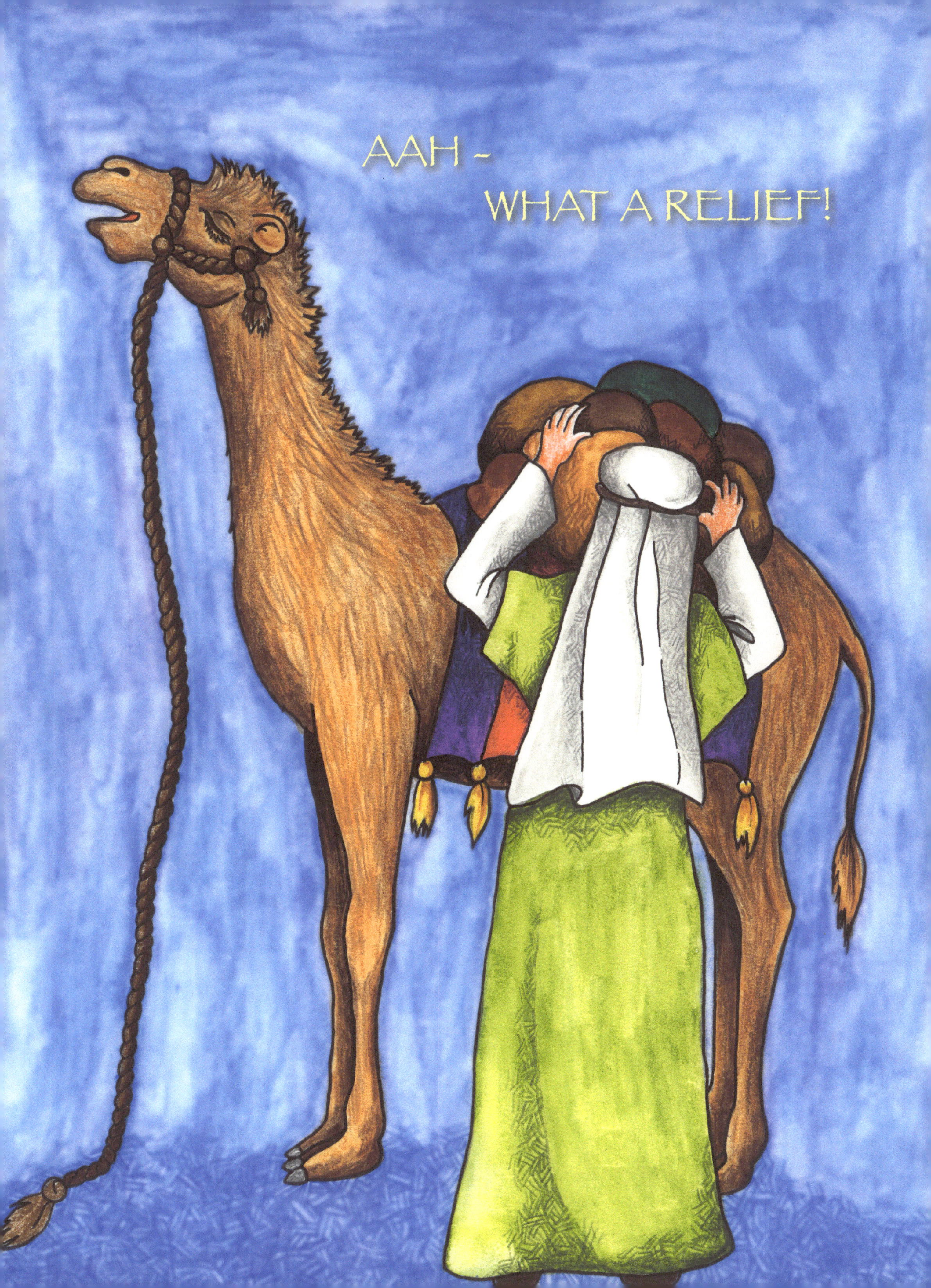
AAH -
WHAT A RELIEF!

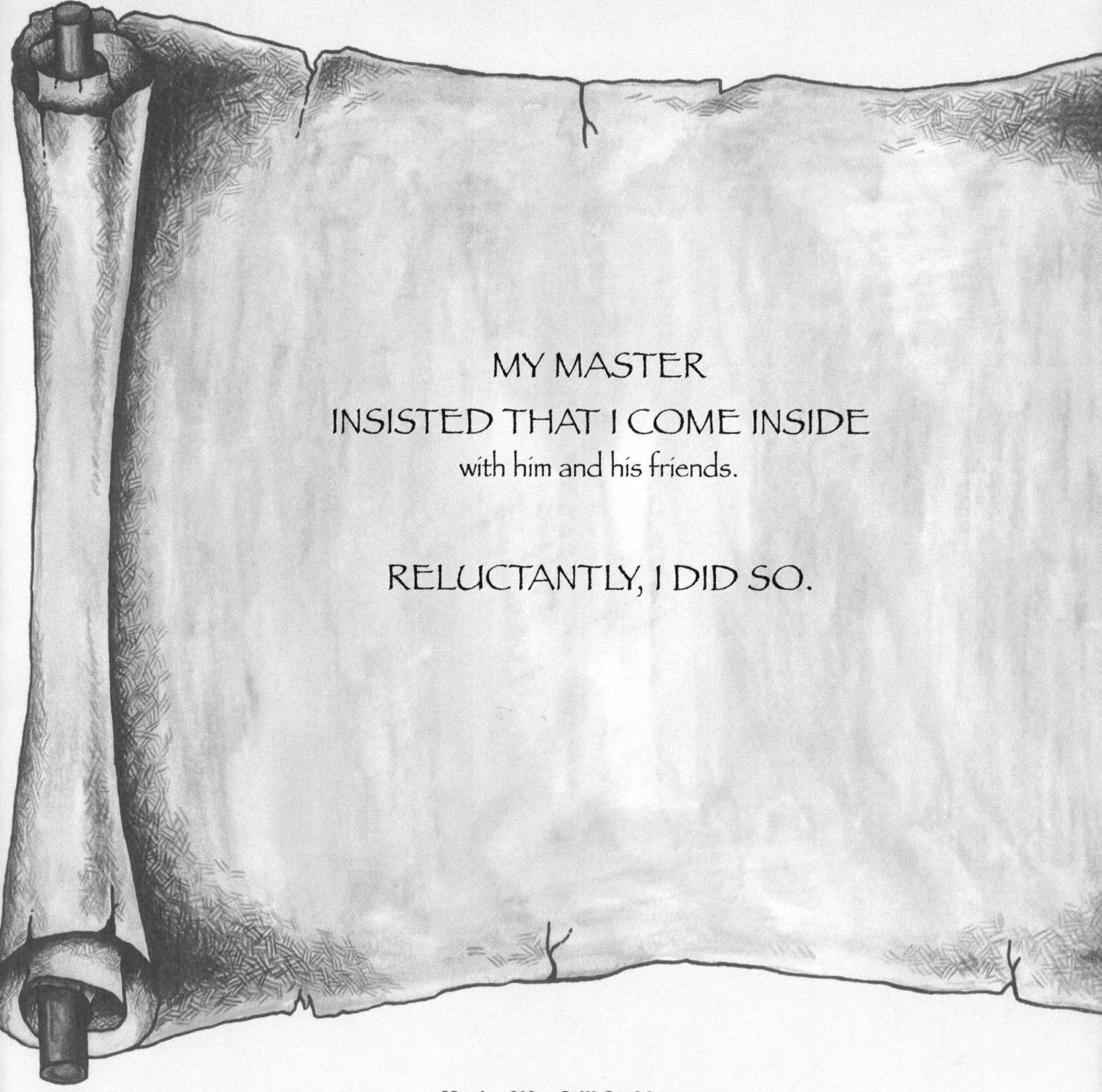

MY MASTER
INSISTED THAT I COME INSIDE
with him and his friends.

RELUCTANTLY, I DID SO.

Xavier Was Still Stubborn

We don't always know what is best for us when our pride stands in the way. Often times
God uses other people to help us see His truth. Xavier went in to meet Jesus only because his good master insisted.

The Bible says, "Do not be wise in your own eyes." *(Proverbs 3: 7)*
"The fear of the Lord is the beginning of wisdom." *(Psalm 111: 10)*

"If we claim to be without sin we deceive ourselves and the truth is not in us. If we confess
our sins, he is faithful and just and will forgive us our sins and purify us from all unrighteousness." *(1 John 1: 8, 9)*

We must admit our sins (faults or short comings) and ask God to forgive us (repent).
Then we need to let God show us how to live and change.

"Trust in the Lord with all your heart and lean not on your own understanding.
In all your ways acknowledge him, and he will make your paths straight." *(Proverbs 3: 5, 6)*

HE MADE ME COME INSIDE

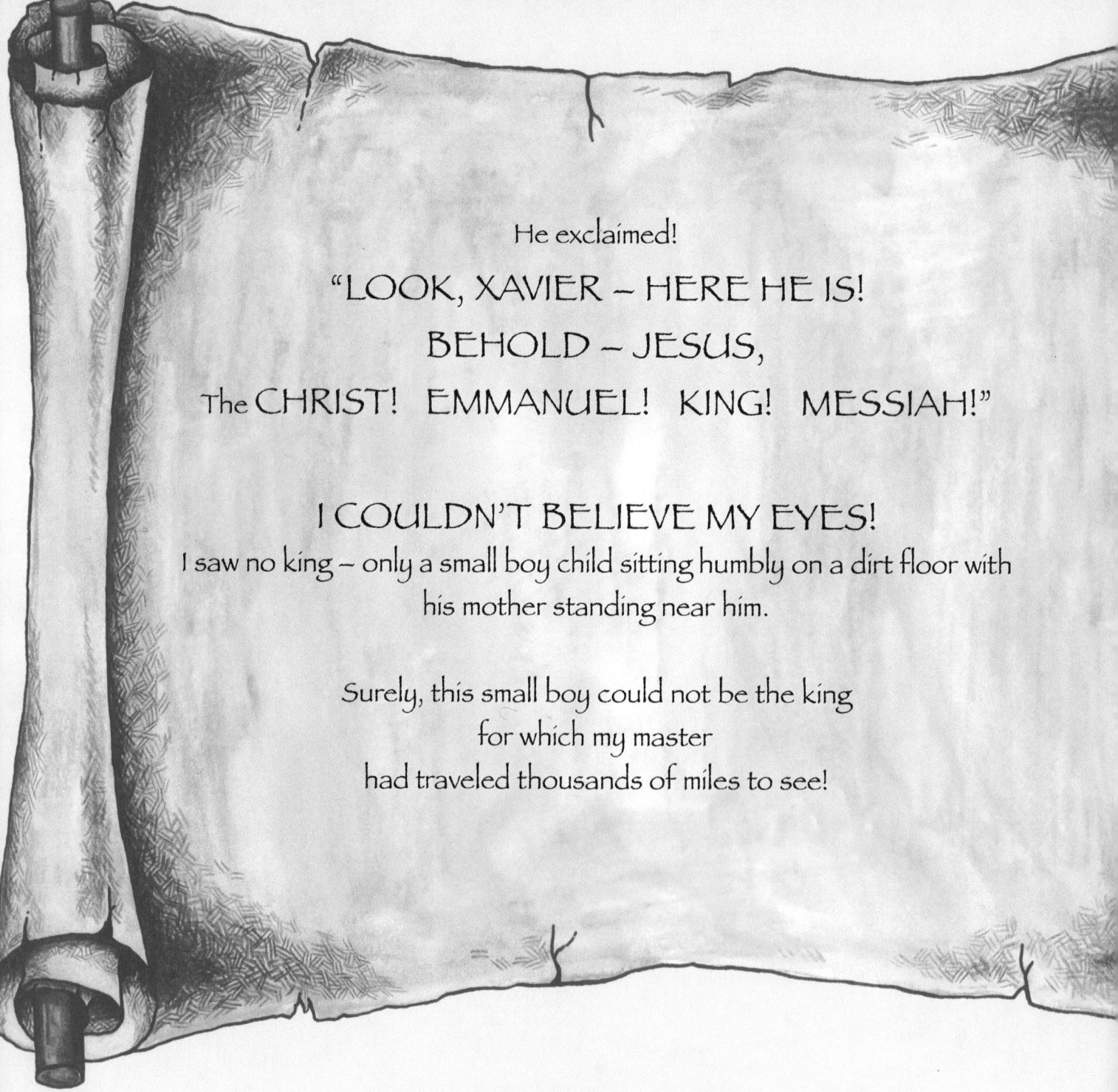

He exclaimed!
"LOOK, XAVIER – HERE HE IS!
BEHOLD – JESUS,
The CHRIST!   EMMANUEL!   KING!   MESSIAH!"

I COULDN'T BELIEVE MY EYES!
I saw no king – only a small boy child sitting humbly on a dirt floor with his mother standing near him.

Surely, this small boy could not be the king
for which my master
had traveled thousands of miles to see!

Xavier's Heart was Filled with Unbelief

Xavier thought, "This small boy couldn't be a king!" It just didn't make sense to him.
Sometimes we can miss coming to Jesus because we expect him to be someone different than he is.

Who is Jesus?
The name Jesus in Hebrew means Savior.

The Bible says Jesus is God's Son sent to earth to save us from our sins and make it possible for us to live with Him forever.

"For God so loved the world that he gave his one and only son, that whoever believes in him shall not perish but have eternal life. For God did not send his son into the world to condemn the world, but to save the world through him." *(John 3: 16, 17)*

Jesus said: "I am the way and the truth and the life, no one comes to the Father except through me." *(John 14: 6)*

I SAW NO KING!

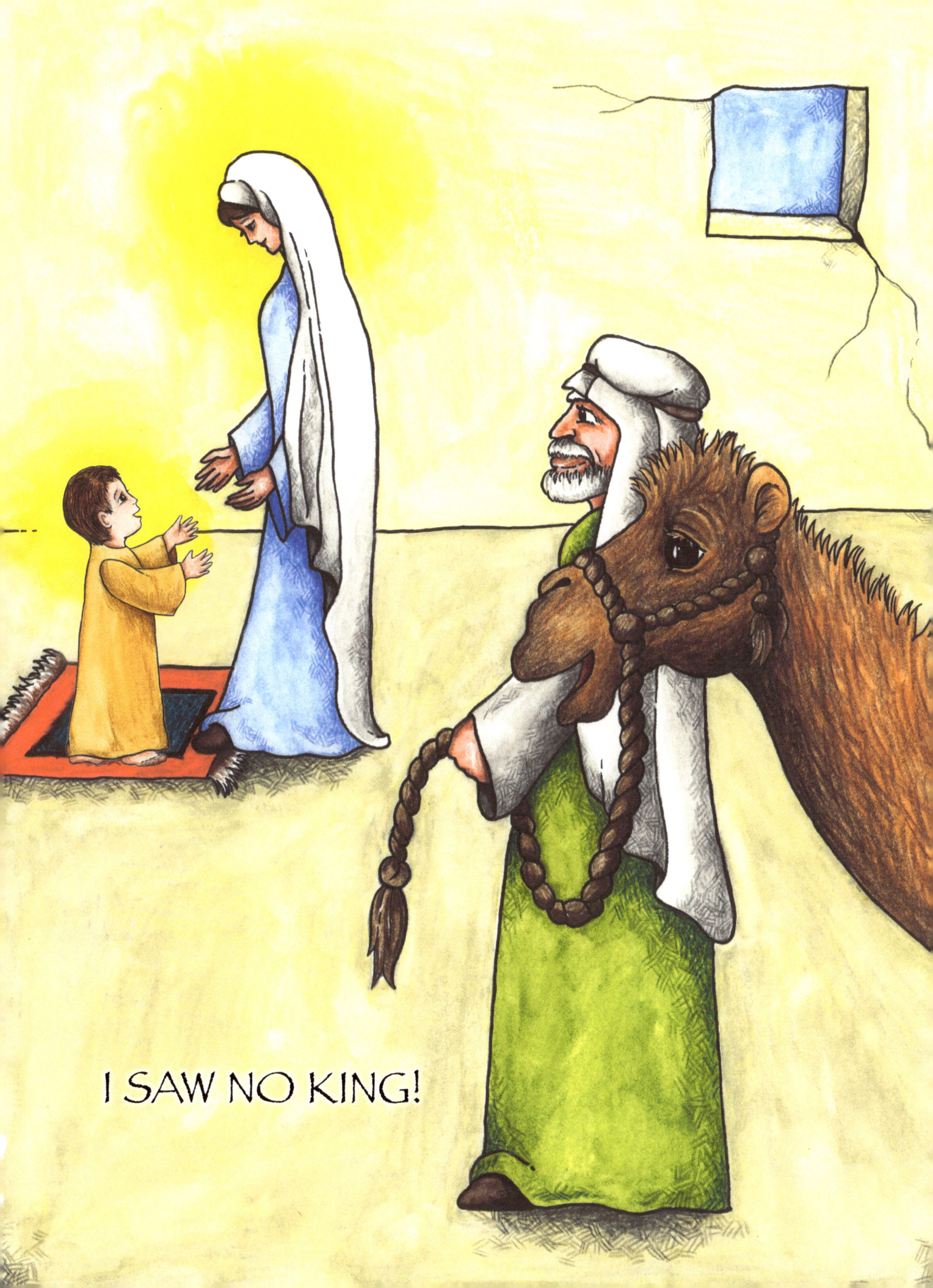

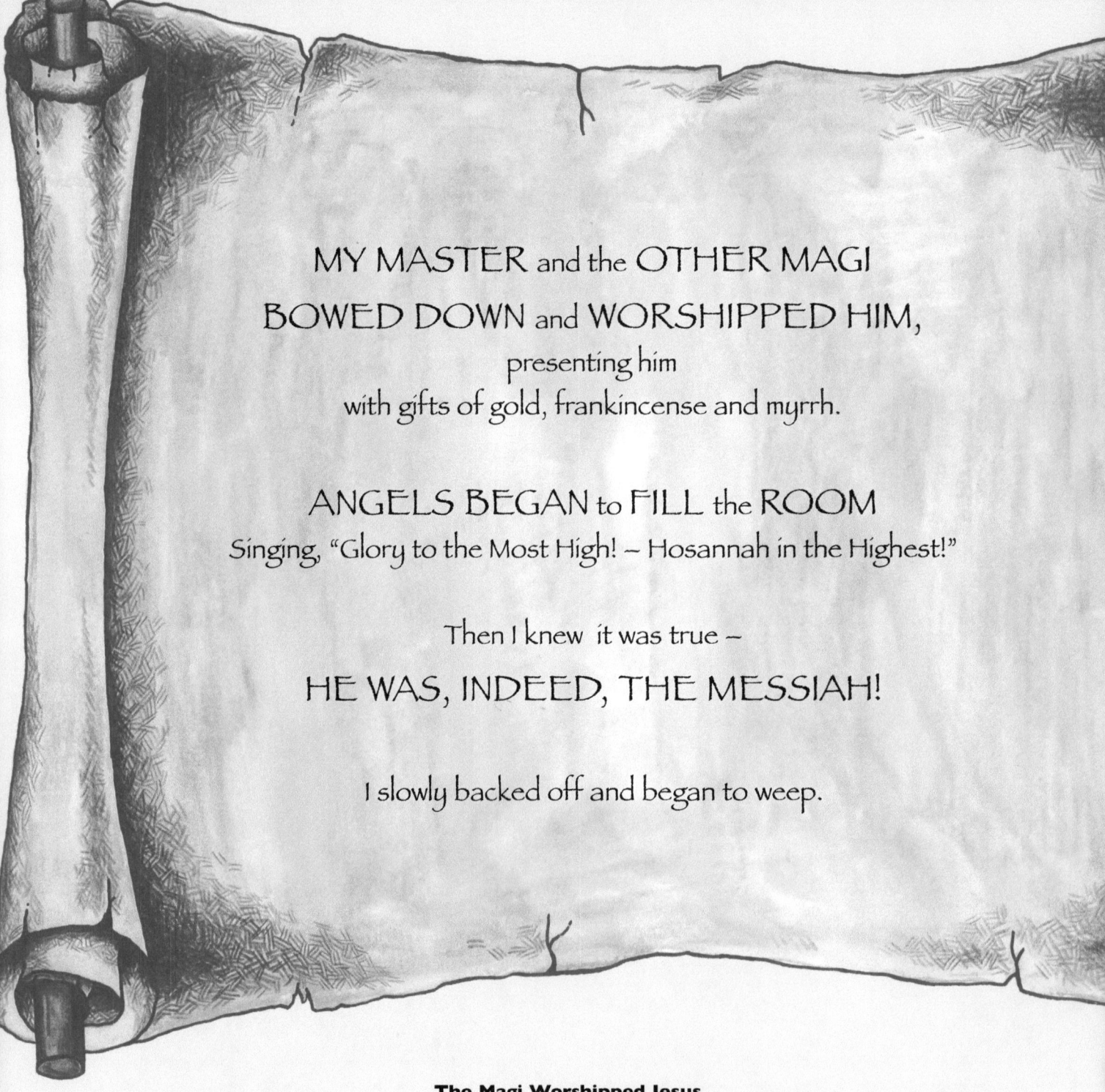

MY MASTER and the OTHER MAGI
BOWED DOWN and WORSHIPPED HIM,
presenting him
with gifts of gold, frankincense and myrrh.

ANGELS BEGAN to FILL the ROOM
Singing, "Glory to the Most High! – Hosannah in the Highest!"

Then I knew it was true –

HE WAS, INDEED, THE MESSIAH!

I slowly backed off and began to weep.

The Magi Worshipped Jesus

The Bible says, "...They went on their way, and the star they had seen in the east went ahead of them until it stopped over the place where the child was. When they saw the star, they were overjoyed. On coming to the house, they saw the child with his mother Mary, and they bowed down and worshipped him. Then they opened their treasures and presented him with gifts of gold and of incense and of myrrh." *(Matthew 2: 9–11)*

About Angels

Angels played an important part in announcing to us the arrival of Christ and in telling us who he is.

An angel named Gabriel appeared to Mary and told her she would have a son whose father would be God. He told her to name him Jesus. (Read about it from God's word in *Luke 1: 26–38*)

Angels announced the birth of Jesus to Shepherds. " ... The angel said to them, 'Do not be afraid. I bring you good news of great joy that will be for all people. Today in the town of David a Savior has been born to you; he is Christ the Lord.' " *(Luke 2: 10-11)*

IT WAS TRUE – HE WAS THE MESSIAH!

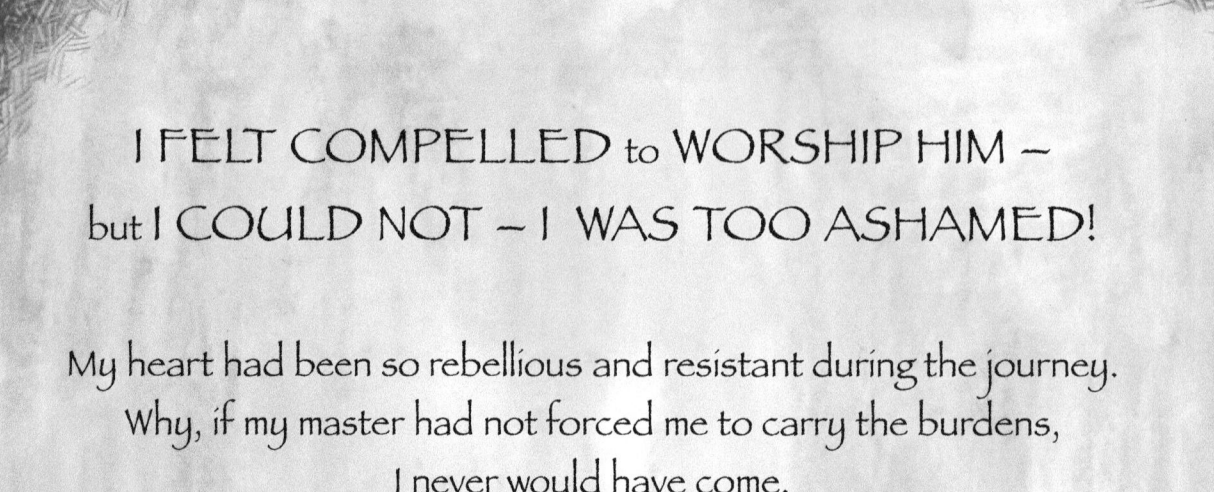

I FELT COMPELLED to WORSHIP HIM –
but I COULD NOT – I WAS TOO ASHAMED!

My heart had been so rebellious and resistant during the journey.
Why, if my master had not forced me to carry the burdens,
I never would have come.

I was thinking,

"I CERTAINLY am UNWORTHY to be in the
PRESENCE of THIS MAGNIFICENT ONE!"

No One is Worthy

Sometimes we feel we're not good enough for God to want anything to do with us.
The truth is, we're not! The Bible tells us, "All have sinned and fall short of the glory of God." *(Romans 3: 23)*

We All Need a Savior

The Bible says, "For the wages of sin is death." *(Romans 6: 23)*
Jesus is the only one who is able to save us from the death we deserve because of our sin. We can't earn it.
It's a gift we have to accept from Him. (Read *Ephesians 2: 8-9*)

"It is by the name of Jesus Christ of Nazareth ... salvation is found in no one else, for there is no other
name under heaven given to men by which we must be saved." *(Acts 4: 10-12)*

We are so precious to Jesus because He created us. He knows each of us and He calls us by name.

Jesus wants us to come to Him.

I FELT SO ASHAMED!

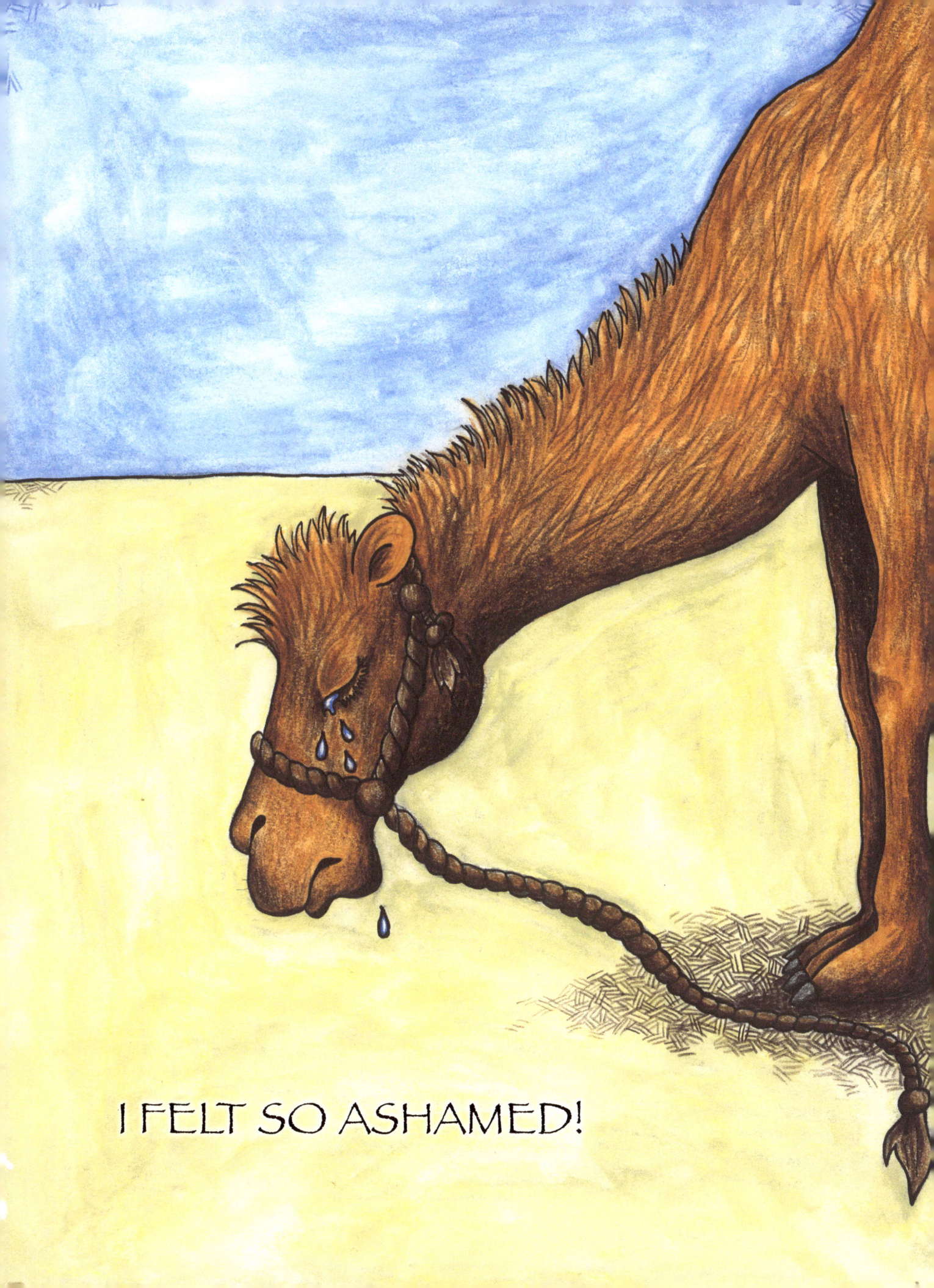

Just then, the child they called

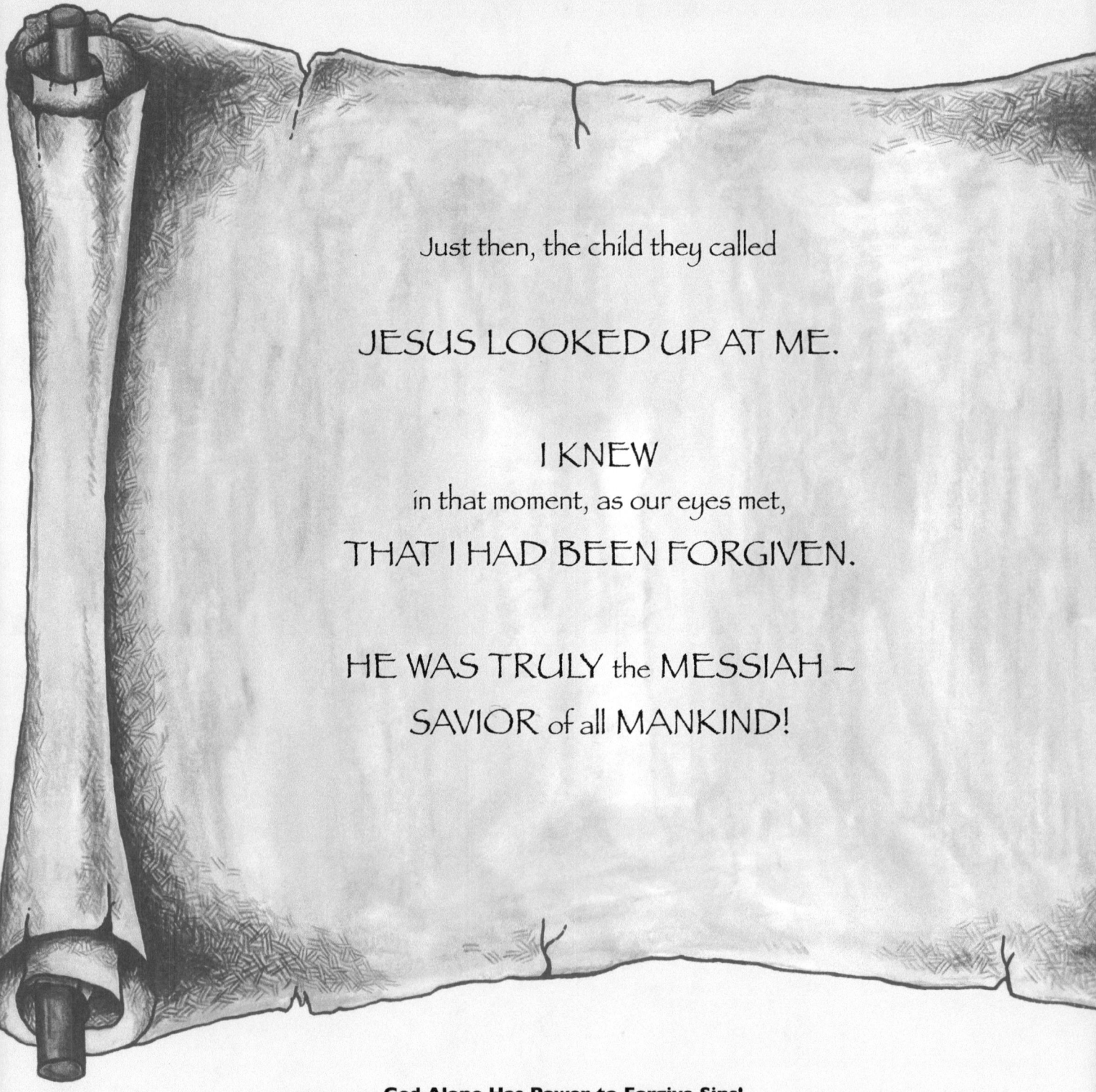

JESUS LOOKED UP AT ME.

I KNEW
in that moment, as our eyes met,
THAT I HAD BEEN FORGIVEN.

HE WAS TRULY the MESSIAH —
SAVIOR of all MANKIND!

God Alone Has Power to Forgive Sins!

The Bible confirms over and over again that Jesus is God. In Mark 2: 1-12 we read about a paralyzed man that was brought to Jesus by his friends who believed that Jesus could heal him.

The Bible says, "When Jesus saw their faith, he said to the paralytic, 'Son, your sins are forgiven.' Now some teachers of the law were sitting there, thinking to themselves, 'Why does this fellow talk like that? He's blaspheming! Who can forgive sins but God alone?'

Immediately Jesus knew in his spirit that this was what they were thinking in their hearts, and he said to them, 'Why are you thinking these things? Which is easier: to say to the paralytic, your sins are forgiven, or to say, Get up, take up your mat and walk? But that you may know that the Son of Man has authority on earth to forgive sins …' He said, . . . 'I tell you, get up, take your mat and go home.'

He (the paralyzed man) got up, took his mat and walked out in full view of them all. This amazed everyone and they praised God saying, 'We have never seen anything like this!'"

HE FORGAVE ME!

Just then my master came and beckoned to me,

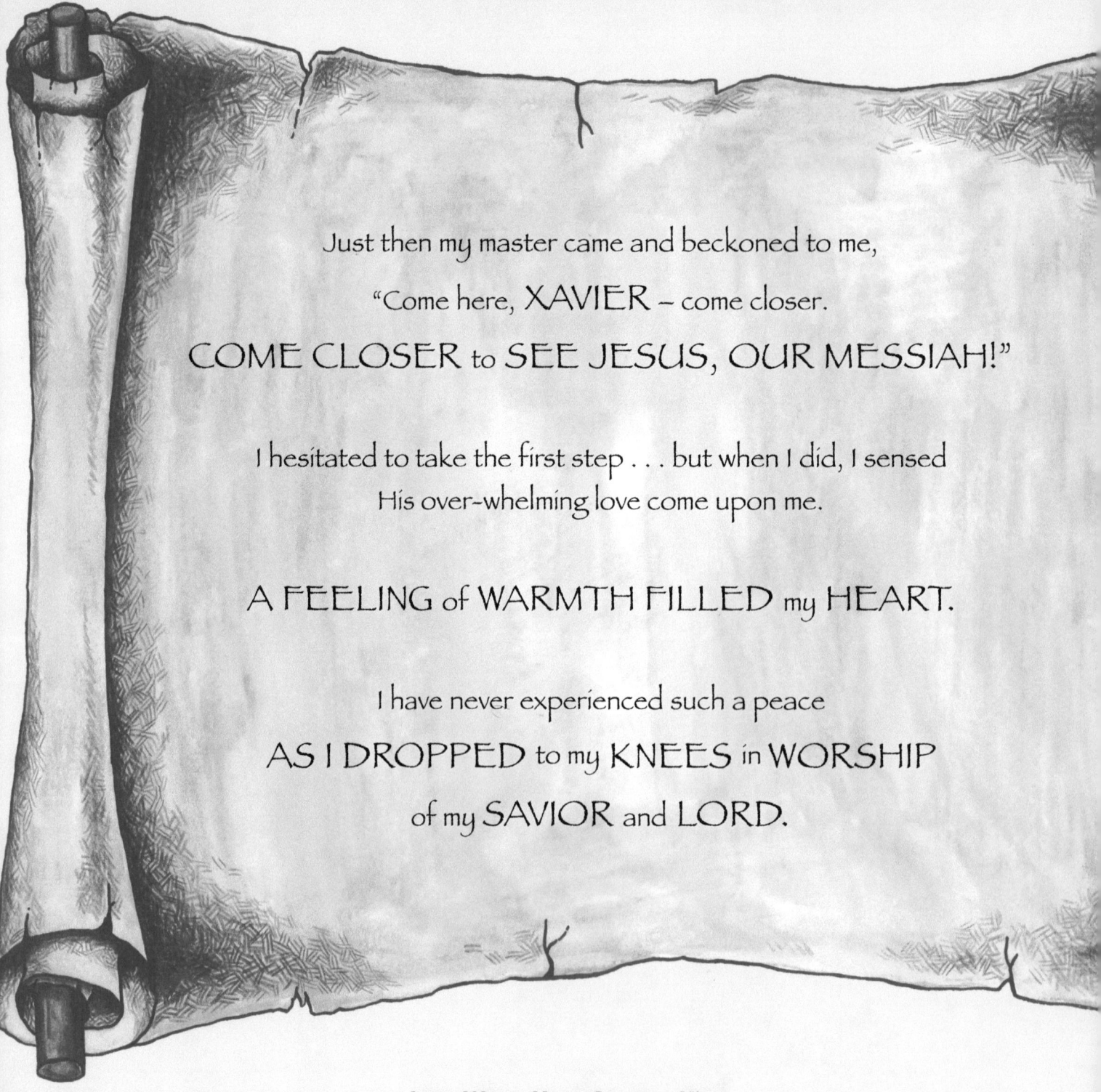

"Come here, XAVIER – come closer.

COME CLOSER to SEE JESUS, OUR MESSIAH!"

I hesitated to take the first step . . . but when I did, I sensed
His over-whelming love come upon me.

A FEELING of WARMTH FILLED my HEART.

I have never experienced such a peace
AS I DROPPED to my KNEES in WORSHIP
of my SAVIOR and LORD.

Jesus Wants Us to Come to Him

In God's Word, the Bible, we learn that each of us were created by Him
and that He intended for us to have a close, personal friendship with Him. It is our sin that separates us from God.

The Bible tells us all we have to do is come to Jesus, ask Him to forgive us and He will.
He will teach us how to follow Him, if we are willing, and we will have a peace that passes understanding.

In Matthew 11: 28-30 Jesus says, "Come to Me, all you who are weary and burdened, and I will give you rest.
Take my yoke upon you and learn from me, for I am gentle and humble in heart, and you will find rest for your souls."

The rest that Jesus promises comes only from knowing Him. It is love, healing, and peace with God.

HIS LOVE FILLED MY HEART

And so it is – what began as the most humiliating
and painful experience of my life, resulted in
my greatest blessing!

I AM FOREVER CHANGED

by

HIS LOVE for ME!

Indeed – I WILL NEVER BE the SAME!

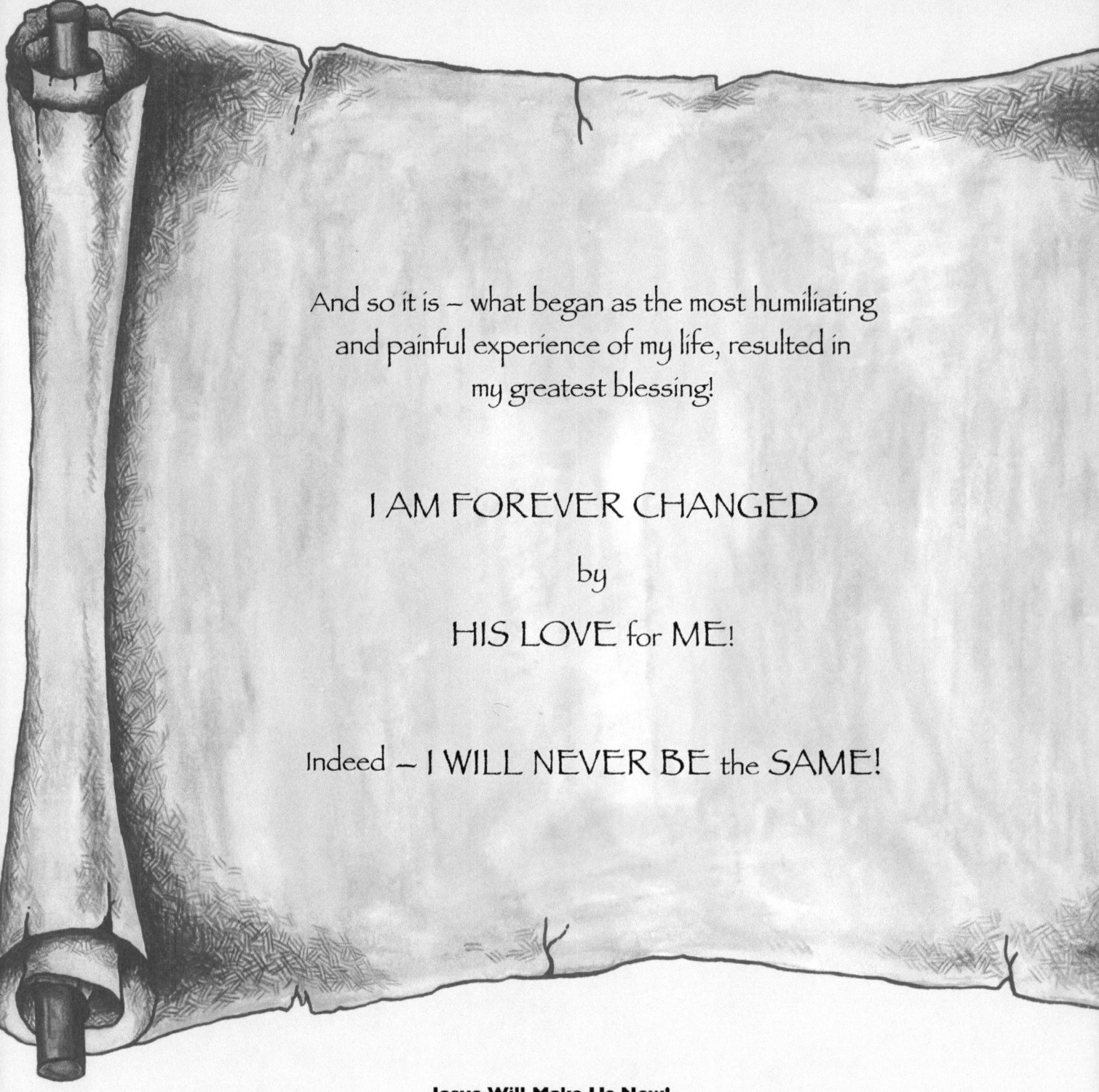

Jesus Will Make Us New!

"Therefore, if anyone is in Christ, he is a new creation; the old is gone, the new is come!" *(2 Corinthians 5:17-18)*

When we come to Jesus, He makes us brand new on the inside. The Holy Spirit gives us new life, and we are not the same anymore.
We are not reformed, rehabilitated, or re-educated – we are recreated in our spirit, living in vital union
with the one who made us, Jesus Christ. *(Read Colossians 2:6,7)*

We are all sinners in need of a savior.
In a way, we are all like Xavier was before he met Jesus. Experiencing the love of Jesus changed Xavier's heart from
selfish, stubborn, and proud to warm, loving, and generous.

Asking Jesus into your heart will make you "brand new" too, and you will be able to say as Xavier
did, "I am forever changed by His love for me - - Indeed, I will never be the same!"

I WILL NEVER BE THE SAME!

WELCOME
(Free Carrots)

Come to Jesus

Jesus prayed for future believers: "Righteous Father ... I have made you known to them and will continue to make you known in order that the love you have for me may be in them and I myself may be in them." (*John 17: 25-26*)

Jesus said: "Ask and it will be given to you; seek and you will find; knock and the door will be opened unto you. For everyone who asks receives, he who seeks finds; and to him who knocks, the door will be opened." (*Luke 11: 9-10*)

"Here I am. I stand at the door and knock. If anyone hears my voice and opens the door I will come in ..." (*Revelation 3: 20*)

You Can Ask Him Now!

"Jesus, I believe that you are the Messiah, Savior of the world. You came to save me from my sin.

I believe you created me and know all about me – You know every wrong thought I've ever had – and every wrong thing I've ever done.

Please forgive me, Jesus, and make me brand new on the inside. Help me follow you for the rest of my life."

Follow Jesus

"Every one who trusts in him will never be put to shame." (*Romans 10: 10-13*)

The Bible says: "Now you must rid yourselves of all such things as these: anger, rage, malice, slander, and filthy language from your lips.

Do not lie to each other, since you have taken off your old self with its practices and have put on the new self, which is being renewed in the image of its Creator.

Here there is no Greek or Jew, circumcised or uncircumcised, barbarian, Scythian, slave or free, but Christ is all, and is in all.

Therefore, as God's chosen people, holy and dearly loved, clothe yourselves with compassion, kindness, humility, gentleness, and patience.

Bear with each other and forgive whatever grievances you may have against one another.

Forgive as the Lord forgave you. And over all these virtues put on love, which binds them all together in perfect unity.

Let the peace of Christ rule in your hearts, since as members of one body you were called to peace.

And be thankful." (*Colossians 3: 8-15*)

Printed in the USA
CPSIA information can be obtained
at www.ICGtesting.com
JSHW041756130923
48300JS00001B/1